The Stuarts

of

Highcliffe

Robert Franklin

A British Library Cataloguing in Publication Data
A catalogue record for this book is available from the British Library.

Published by Natula Publications
5 St Margaret's Avenue, Christchurch, Dorset BH23 1JD

Printed By Redwood Books Limited
Kennet Way, Trowbridge, Wiltshire BA14 8RN

Front Cover Illustration :

        Portrait of Louisa, Marchioness of Waterford
        by George Frederic Watts
        by kind permission of Sir Andrew Duff Gordon, Bart.

Back Cover Illustration :

        'Spy' cartoon of 1899 of the then
        Major Edward Stuart Wortley.

Inside Front Cover Illustration :

        'High Cliff'
        an engraving by W.Watts
        of a drawing by H.R.Callander, published in 1784

Contents

List of Illustrations

PREFACE

THIS BOOK is a collection of short accounts of the 3rd Earl of Bute and those of his descendants who can be counted, with him, as having belonged at Highcliffe. Some of the family may be well enough known already: there are biographies of Lord Stuart de Rothesay and Lady Canning; and much has been written about Lord Bute, himself, and Lady Waterford. But there are gaps in the story of the Stuarts of Highcliffe, and these accounts fill at least some of them.

I have tried to keep a balance between telling a story and presenting facts, and so I have reserved references and footnotes chiefly for direct quotations and matters that seemed to me to call for authentication. Otherwise, sources are indicated in the text, for instance by the mention of Navy and Army Lists. In the case of Lord Stuart de Rothesay and Lady Canning, additional references are listed in the biographies.

I acknowledge gratefully the help I have had from individuals and the staff of libraries, museums, etc. Among the individuals, there are the late Marquess of Bute; Dr.R.Custance, Archivist, Winchester College; Mr Peter Donnelly, Assistant Keeper, King's Own Royal Regiment Museum, Lancaster; Sir Andrew Duff Gordon, Bart.; Brigadier A.I.H.Fyfe, Regimental Secretary, Somerset Light Infantry, Taunton; Mr A.D.K.Hawkyard, Archivist, Harrow School; Mr Jim Hunter, Curator, The Red House Museum, Christchurch; Lord Joicey; Major P.A. Lewis, Regimental Archivist, Grenadier Guards; Ms Sarah Medlam, Deputy Curator of Furniture and Woodwork, Victoria and Albert Museum; Mrs Sue Newman; and Major W.H.White, Curator, Regimental Museum, the Duke of Cornwall's Light Infantry, Bodmin. It would be invidious to mention any one individual from Highcliffe, so many people here having helped me in one way or another.

Among the libraries from which I have had help are: the British Library (the Newspaper Library and the Oriental and India Office Collection);

Cambridge University Library; Edinburgh University Library; the Foreign and Commonwealth Office Library; Guildhall Library, London; the Harriet Irving Library, University of New Brunswick; the Hartley Library, University of Southampton; the National Art Library, Victoria and Albert Museum; and Portsmouth Central Library.

Equally important sources of advice and information have been: Dorset County Record Office; Hampshire County Record Office; the House of Lords Record Office; the National Army Museum (the Reading Room and the Department of Archives); the National Maritime Museum, Greenwich; the Office for National Statistics (General Register Office); the Public Record Office; the Royal Green Jackets Museum, Winchester; the Royal Naval Museum, Portsmouth; the Somerset Military Museum, Taunton; and the West Yorkshire Archive Service, Leeds District Archives.

Queen Victoria's Journal and letters to Queen Victoria from Lord and Lady Canning are quoted by gracious permission of Her Majesty The Queen. The quotations from Edinburgh University Library manuscripts are made by permission from the Library, and those from the *Chronicle of the King's Royal Rifle Corps* with permission from the Royal Green Jackets Museum. The Quotations from *The Stanleys of Alderly* are made by permission of the Peters, Fraser and Dunlop Group Limited, on behalf of the estate of Nancy Mitford (Copyright: Estate of Nancy Mitford), and the extract from the *River War* is reproduced by permission of Curtis Brown Limited, on behalf of the estate of Sir Winston Churchill (Copyright: Estate of Sir Winston Churchill). The verse from Sir Henry Newbolt's poem *Vitaï Lampada* is reprinted by permission of his grandson, Mr Peter Newbolt, who holds the copyright.

It is a pleasure, finally, to thank Mrs Jane Martin, of Natula Publications, for the way in which she has seen the book through the process of publication, I have avoided jargon and cliché as much as possible, but I can only describe Natula Limited as user-friendly.

Highcliffe, 1998   Robert Franklin

SIMPLIFIED GENEALOGICAL TABLES

TABLE 1

The Earl of Bute and his Children

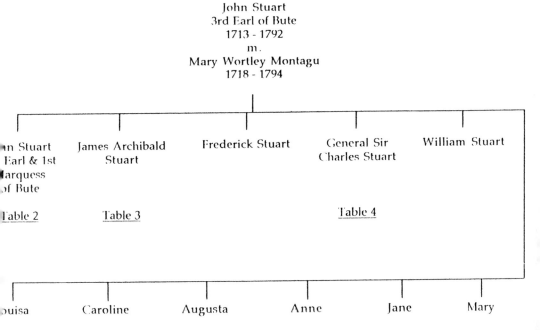

John Stuart
3rd Earl of Bute
1713 - 1792
m.
Mary Wortley Montagu
1718 - 1794

...n Stuart Earl & 1st Marquess of Bute	James Archibald Stuart	Frederick Stuart	General Sir Charles Stuart	William Stuart
Table 2	Table 3		Table 4	

...uisa	Caroline	Augusta	Anne	Jane	Mary

TABLE 2

The 3rd Marquess of Bute

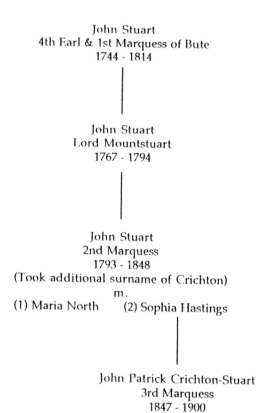

John Stuart
4th Earl & 1st Marquess of Bute
1744 - 1814

John Stuart
Lord Mountstuart
1767 - 1794

John Stuart
2nd Marquess
1793 - 1848
(Took additional surname of Crichton)
m.
(1) Maria North   (2) Sophia Hastings

John Patrick Crichton-Stuart
3rd Marquess
1847 - 1900

TABLE 3

General Edward Stuart Wortley

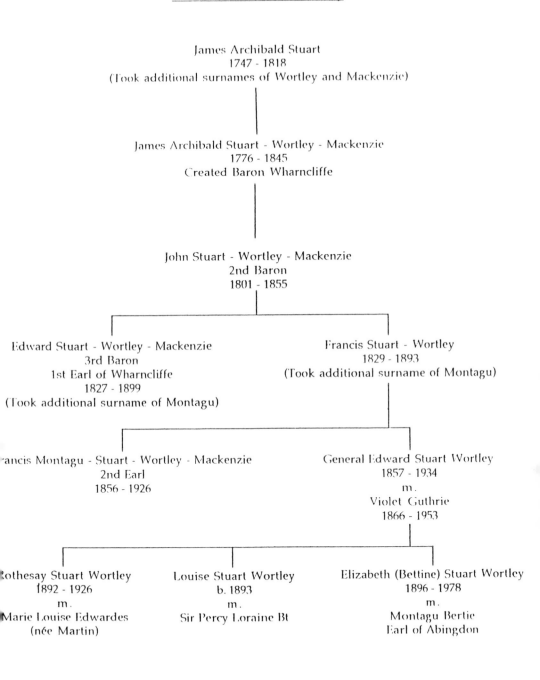

James Archibald Stuart
1747 - 1818
(Took additional surnames of Wortley and Mackenzie)

James Archibald Stuart - Wortley - Mackenzie
1776 - 1845
Created Baron Wharncliffe

John Stuart - Wortley - Mackenzie
2nd Baron
1801 - 1855

Edward Stuart - Wortley - Mackenzie
3rd Baron
1st Earl of Wharncliffe
1827 - 1899
(Took additional surname of Montagu)

Francis Stuart - Wortley
1829 - 1893
(Took additional surname of Montagu)

Francis Montagu - Stuart - Wortley - Mackenzie
2nd Earl
1856 - 1926

General Edward Stuart Wortley
1857 - 1934
m.
Violet Guthrie
1866 - 1953

Rothesay Stuart Wortley
1892 - 1926
m.
Marie Louise Edwardes
(née Martin)

Louise Stuart Wortley
b. 1893
m.
Sir Percy Loraine Bt

Elizabeth (Bettine) Stuart Wortley
1896 - 1978
m.
Montagu Bertie
Earl of Abingdon

TABLE 4

General Sir Charles Stuart and his Descendants

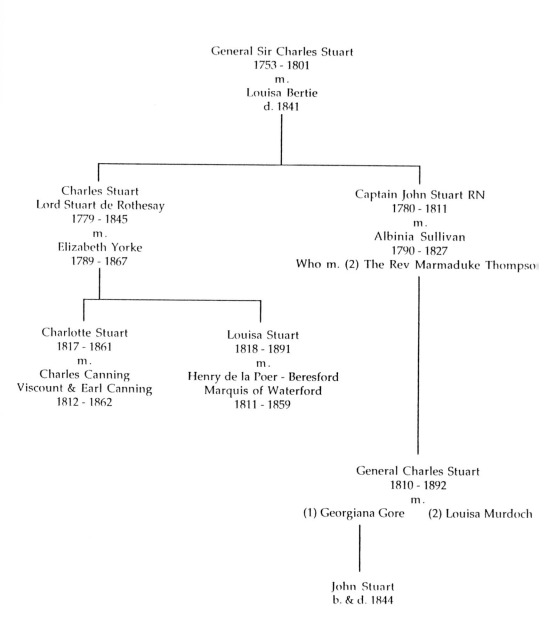

General Sir Charles Stuart
1753 - 1801
m.
Louisa Bertie
d. 1841

Charles Stuart
Lord Stuart de Rothesay
1779 - 1845
m.
Elizabeth Yorke
1789 - 1867

Captain John Stuart RN
1780 - 1811
m.
Albinia Sullivan
1790 - 1827
Who m. (2) The Rev Marmaduke Thompso

Charlotte Stuart
1817 - 1861
m.
Charles Canning
Viscount & Earl Canning
1812 - 1862

Louisa Stuart
1818 - 1891
m.
Henry de la Poer - Beresford
Marquis of Waterford
1811 - 1859

General Charles Stuart
1810 - 1892
m.
(1) Georgiana Gore   (2) Louisa Murdoch

John Stuart
b. & d. 1844

INTRODUCTION

ONE DAY IN 1885, The Prince of Wales, later King Edward VII, suggested to Louisa, Marchioness of Waterford and chatelaine of Highcliffe Castle, that the place should go to a certain member of her husband's family, after her death. Lady Waterford respectfully demurred. Highcliffe, she explained to His Royal Highness, was 'a Stuart place'.[1]

It had been a Stuart place since 1770, or thereabouts, when Lady Waterford's great-grandfather, John Stuart, 3rd Earl of Bute, on a botanical expedition, found himself on the cliff-top overlooking Christchurch Bay, and was charmed by the scene before him. The story is that he decided, there and then, to make his home there, and that he would not leave the spot until Robert Adam, the architect, arrived to begin work on his project.[2] He called his new house High Cliff.

Lord Bute's fourth and favourite son, Lieutenant-General the Honourable Sir Charles Stuart, inherited High Cliff, but he was forced by landslips to demolish the house, and he chose to sell the greater part of the estate. Years later, however, General Stuart's elder son, Lord Stuart de Rothesay, bought back the land that had been sold, and built the house that became known as Highclifffe Castle.

Lord Stuart de Rothesay had no son to inherit his title and property, but he had two daughters, Charlotte, Viscountess and later Countess Canning, and Louisa, Marchioness of Waterford, neither of whom had children. The house passed to Lady Stuart de Rothesay and then to Lady Waterford, who bequeathed it to a cousin, Major-General the Honourable Edward Stuart Wortley. General Stuart Wortley had a son, Rothesay, and two daughters, Louise, who married Sir Percy Loraine, Bart., and Elizabeth, or Bettine, who married Montagu Bertie, 8th Earl of Abingdon. Rothesay died before he could inherit the house, and it was bought from his widow by Lord Abingdon, who was its last private owner.

The house was called simply Highcliffe for many years, while the nearby village, grown from a hamlet known as Slop Pond, was called Newtown. Gradually, however, the place took over the name of the house. In 1862 a new parish was carved out of the Parish of Christchurch

1

and called Highcliffe, and in 1892 Newton Post Office, for which confusion with other places called Newtown had become a problem, was officially renamed Highcliffe Post Office. It was then, at the turn of the century, in order to avoid further confusion, that the house became known as Highcliffe Castle.

Two other members of the family must be mentioned here. They are Lord Stuart de Rothesay's brother, Captain John Stuart, R.N., and Captain Stuart's son, General Charles Stuart.

THE EARL OF BUTE

LORD BUTE was descended on his father's side from an illegitimate son of King Robert II of Scotland, and his mother was the daughter of the Ist Duke of Argyll. He was born in Scotland in 1713 but brought up in England from the age of ten, when his father died and he succeeded to the earldom. He was at school at Eton, and at university not in England or Scotland but in Holland. He was an intelligent young man with wide interests, and he was to play a notable part in the nation's intellectual and cultural life, though this has always attracted less attention than his role in public and political affairs.

He fell in love with Mary Wortley Montagu, daughter of the celebrated Lady Mary Wortley Montagu, and she with him, but Lady Mary disapproved. This formidable feminist, who had dispensed with her husband, was sceptical of romantic notions of marriage; and, to make matters worse, the Wortley Montagus were rich and Bute was not. However, Mary showed the spirit that Lady Mary had shown in her own matrimonial affairs, and she and Bute were married in 1736. Edward Wortley Montagu, Lady Mary's estranged husband and Mary's father, disapproved of the match, too, but he appeared at the ceremony to give the bride away.

Bute sat in Parliament at Westminster as a Scottish Representative Peer for the four years that followed his marriage, but he did not take much part in its proceedings, and he may not have been disappointed when he lost his seat. He spent the next five years in Scotland, chiefly at Mount Stuart, his home on the Isle of Bute, where he and his growing family could live economically but still in some style,, and he could happily pursue his own interests. Then he felt the lure of London, and he returned to England and set himself up in a modest establishment at Twickenham.

Fortunately for him, an active mind was not the only asset that he had to set against his lack of funds: he had good looks and charm, and it so happened, at a time when private theatricals were much in vogue, that he had a talent for acting. He was, in fact, as well equipped for London society as for solitude on a Scottish island.

The turning point in his life was a chance meeting with Frederick, Prince of Wales, at Egham Races, soon after his return to the south. Rain had interrupted the day's programme, and cards were proposed for the Prince's entertainment. For some reason, the royal party required another member for the purpose, and it was Bute, spied among the other race-goers, who saved the situation.[3]

Frederick took to him at once, and invited him to Leicester House and Cliveden, where he found such favour with Augusta, Princess of Wales, that tongues began to wag. It was not long before he was given a post in the royal household, and not long again before Frederick died, leaving Augusta, who felt alone and vulnerable, to care for their thirteen year old son, George, the new heir to the throne. Augusta turned more and more to Bute for advice and support, and tongues wagged faster and more furiously. It was generally believed that they were lovers, but it is by no means certain that they were.

More remarkable than Bute's relationship with Augusta was his relationship with George, which was one of mutual devotion, deepened when Bute became George's private tutor at Augusta's behest - regardless of the fact that the future king's education was officially in other hands. A personal relationship in history must often be a matter of speculation, but in this case a collection of private letters makes guesswork unnecessary: Bute is shown to have been a wily courtier, intelligent, well-informed, shrewd, fond of his young charge and aware of his responsibility towards him, but heavy and sententious; and George is disclosed as a naive young man, unsure of himself, anxious to please and fulsome, though sometimes touching in his idealism.[4] George refers to Bute throughout the correspondence as his 'dear friend'.

Bute is said to have been an ambitious man, but he did not show much ambition until he was taken up by Frederick, and it would have been strange if he had not wanted to make the most of royal favour. Whatever was the truth of the matter, his position as confidant and counsellor to the heir to the throne and his mother, in an age in which kings still had the right to choose their own ministers, and at a time at which it was expected that the throne would soon become vacant, was one of considerable influence.

4

There is no doubt that he was an unpopular man, and one reason for this was that he was considered to be too ambitious. But there were more important reasons, the most fundamental of which was that he was an outsider who had broken into a charmed circle: he could not have been more of an outsider than he was as a Scot - "Scotchman" at this time had become little less than a synonym for undesirable immigrant'[5] - and he could not have broken further into the charmed circle than the foot of the throne.

George succeeded to the throne as King George III in 1760. He had already made it clear that he intended to have Bute as his chief minister, but he could not afford to act in too arbitrary a manner. He could and did make a place for his friend in the Cabinet by inducing one of the two Secretaries of State to resign, by means of a generous pension, but then he had to bide his time. Eventually, however, without the need for further machinations, first the other Secretary of State and then the Prime Minister, himself, the Duke of Newcastle, resigned. Bute's hour had come.

Much has been written about Bute's premiership, which began in May 1762 and ended only eleven months later in April 1763, but the story can be made brief. Bute had few friends and many enemies by this time: though he had charm if he cared to use it, he had no man-management skills; and he did not understand the art of the possible.

He brought the Seven Years War to an end, on perfectly satisfactory terms, but he allowed the credit that he deserved to elude him. He was inept enough, when the Exchequer needed funds, to force a tax on cider through Parliament, in spite of a public outcry, simply because an existing tax on beer made it seem logical. Much continued to be made of the fact that he was a Scot and of his supposed relationship with Augusta, and a rumour that he was encouraging the King to take more power into his own hands added fuel to the flames.

The opposition to him in Parliament was merciless, and he was vilified and abused everywhere. A mob attacked his carriage as he was driving to the Opening of Parliament in November 1762, and it was fortunate for him that there were soldiers at hand to protect him. It was not the first or the last time that such treatment was meted out to a politician, but it was too much for Bute. His health began to suffer, and he resigned.

John Stuart, 3rd Earl of Bute
by Sir Joshua Reynolds
By courtesy of the National Portrait Gallery, London

George had already begun to grow out of his relationship with Bute by this time: experience had given him confidence; and he was married. And now his new Prime Minister, George Grenville, told him that the less he and his colleagues heard of the favourite in future the better pleased they would be. Bute would dearly have loved to be back on his old footing with the King, but things were never to be quite the same again, in spite of the dark suspicions harboured by many inside and outside the charmed circle. Ironically, the special friendship that was so precious to Bute continued to be held against him long after there had ceased to be anything special about it.[6]

When he had finally to face the fact that his day was over, he was bitterly unhappy. He felt, not without reason, that he had been unjustly treated by the country at large, and he could not help feeling, perhaps with less reason, that even the King had failed him. He spent some time abroad, part of it with his son Charles, of whom he was particularly fond; and it was when he returned to England that he built High Cliff, which was to be his retreat in this country. He had become a rich man, Mary having inherited a fortune from her father, and the house was large and grand - though not the largest or most grand of his homes - and it was designed and furnished with his special interests in mind. For the rest of his life, he was as happy at High Cliff as he was anywhere.

Bute was fortunate to be able to retire from public life to a life that offered as much that was interesting and absorbing. He had 'the inestimable asset of serious intellectual pursuits'.[7] Botany was the subject to which he contributed most himself, and he is one of those botanists to whom Kew Gardens stand as a memorial. But he contributed as much to other disciplines indirectly, by his patronage of such men as Samuel Johnson, Thomas Sheridan, Allan Ramsay and Robert Adam. And through his involvement in the affairs of the Scottish universities, chiefly in the appointment of professors, he had an influence on what has been called 'the process of defining what Scottish culture was to become'.[8]

He died in London in 1792 and was buried on the Isle of Bute. One account has it that his death was due to an injury to his leg, received when he fell while reaching for a flower at High Cliff two years earlier. 'His enemies said of John Stuart that he had over-reached himself in his public career, as he did when he attempted to grasp at the flower on the steep cliff-side.'[9]

GENERAL SIR CHARLES STUART

GENERAL STUART was born in 1753. The Earl of Bute, his father, was well established in the confidence and affections of the widowed Augusta, Princess Dowager of Wales, and George, her son, the new Prince of Wales, by this time, and his meteoric rise and fall as a politician were still ahead of him. The family was living at Caen Wood House, later to be called Kenwood, but Lord Bute gave up this home in the following year and took a house in South Audley Street and another on Kew Green.

It is said that Charles was sent to Winchester. The school's records show that three of Lord Bute's five sons were there, and they have been identified as Charles and the brothers next before and after him in the family, James Archibald and Frederick. He decided early that the army was to be his career, and he was an ensign in the 37th Regiment at the age of fifteen.

The American War of Independence gave him his first opportunity of distinguishing himself, and he did not waste it. An old soldier, writing of him to a friend in 1777, said 'he is clever, exceedingly intelligent, takes great pains and is as bold as a lion'.[10] And a rarer quality that soon became apparent was a capacity for inspiring confidence, not only in the men whom he led but also in his superior officers: he had charisma.

He was highly critical of the politicians and generals in charge of the war, at least in his letters to his father. Sir Henry Clinton, who was made Commander-in-Chief in 1778, was exempt from the worst of his strictures, however, and the two men were soon on terms of mutual respect, in spite of the differences in age and rank between them. Neither he nor Clinton had any faith in the Secretary of State responsible for American affairs, Lord George Germain, and at the end of 1778, in England whether on leave or as part of his duties, Charles called on Germain to make him aware of the difficulties that the Commander-in-Chief was facing.

Charles had become M.P. for Bossiney in Cornwall in 1776, during his absence in America, the seat being one in which Lord Bute had an interest, and it was as an M.P. and not just as a relatively junior officer that he bearded Germain. All the same, self-assurance was needed, and he demonstrated that this was another of his characteristics. He disagreed with the Minister on at least one important issue in their discussion, and he did not mind saying so.

The war dragged on for another four years, in spite of interventions such as this and in spite of opposition in Parliament, but it so happened that none of these three men saw it through to its bitter end. Charles returned to England with his regiment when it was recalled at the end of 1779. Clinton resigned in 1781 and Germain was discreetly dismissed, with a peerage to console him, in 1782.

On leave in 1778, Charles had married Louisa Bertie, daughter of Lord Vere Bertie, who was a younger son of the 1st Duke of Ancaster. One of their homes was Bure Farm, at Mudeford, near Christchurch, but there was a town house in Whitehall and, also, a grace-and-favour residence in Richmond Park, obtained for them by Lord Bute.

The army kept him unemployed on half-pay between 1779, when he returned from America, and 1793, when the Revolutionary War with France began; and he felt he was being badly treated. During those years, he was involved in politics as an M.P., he travelled abroad and he had the pleasure of watching his two sons, Charles and John, growing up. But, ironically, he was able to make use of his military experience in London in 1780, when the Gordon Riots threatened the city with destruction.

Lord George Gordon was the leader of an extreme Protestant movement. This movement attracted the support of political agitators, and in the end it was taken over by the mob. There was total anarchy in the capital for several days, and the civil authorities seemed to be incapable of doing anything about it until the King, himself, brought them to their senses. Then the army was called in, a proper strategy was devised and order was restored. Charles was an observer of all that transpired, and a plan that he put forward became a crucial part of the successful strategy.[11 & 12]

He was not interested enough in politics to take part in the day to day business of the House of Commons, though he was probably a more or less consistent supporter of William Pitt. In 1790, after fourteen years as M.P. for Bossiney, he stood for Poole, not far from High Cliff, and he was elected but promptly disqualified on the grounds of bribery. Lord Bute and his kinsman the Duke of Argyll saw to it that he was then returned for the Ayr burghs, and six years later, during the Revolutionary War, he stood for Poole again, this time without mishap of any kind, in spite of talk of sharp practice. He was M.P. for Poole from 1796 until his death.

It was in 1792 that Lord Bute died and High Cliff passed to Charles, who disposed of it soon afterwards. It was in 1793 that the Revolutionary War, which led into the Napoleonic Wars, began. And it was in 1794 that Charles was given the command for which he had been waiting.

He was made 'Lieutenant-General in Corsica and in the whole of the Mediterranean except Gibraltar'.[13] A popular uprising had taken place in the French owned island of Corsica, and the insurgents had requested British assistance. Much had already been achieved by the time Charles arrived on the island, but the vital fortress of Calvi had still to be taken. It was accessible only with difficulty at the end of a rocky peninsula, and it was otherwise well protected, but Charles and his second-in-command, Colonel John Moore, invested it on the landward side and a naval force under Captain Horatio Nelson blockaded it from the sea, and the garrison surrendered after a siege of three months.

There was no more action for him until the end of 1796. Then Spain came into the war on the side of France making Britain's military presence in the Mediterranean difficult to maintain, so that Corsica had to be abandoned. This put Portugal at risk of attack. Portugal now requested British assistance, and Charles was given the unenviable task of supplying it. The military situation and the political situation in the country were both confused, and the Secretary at War, Henry Dundas, made matters worse by giving nonsensical instructions. 'I am determined to be guided by your instructions so long as they come within reach of my comprehension', Charles is reputed to have told Dundas on one occasion.[14]

Fortunately, his own men, though few, had been with him in Corsica and were devoted to him. Fortunately, too, there was a naval force at hand, under Admiral Sir John Jervis, who had trounced the Spanish off Cape St. Vincent at the beginning of 1797 - and was raised to the peerage as Earl of St. Vincent. But it was due to his own intelligence and qualities of personality that he was able to bring order out of chaos. In the summer of 1798, he was summoned to London to discuss plans for a new military venture.

Lieutenant-General Sir Charles Stuart
by George Romney
Glasgow Museums: Art Gallery and Museum, Kelvingrove

The plans were agreed, and the operation that followed, later in the year, became his most memorable military exploit. It was the seizure of Minorca, once described as 'the most glorious piece of bluff in the history of the Army'.[15] The Mediterranean had been re-opened to Britain by Nelson's victory over the French at Aboukir Bay, and Minorca was coveted for its strategic position and the naval base of Port Mahon.

The British were outnumbered and outgunned, but the Spanish made the mistake of dividing their force and shutting themselves up in Mahon and Ciudadela, at opposite ends of the island, so that Charles, having placed some of his men where they could prevent reinforcements from moving between the two strongholds, was able to concentrate first on one and then on the other. Mahon, which had a small garrison, surrendered quickly, but Ciudadela was another matter, and it was there that Charles used bluff. He displayed the same men and guns to the enemy at several different places, so as to give the impression of great strength, and went through the motions of preparation for an attack. Then he summoned the garrison to surrender, and though a second summons was necessary a third was not.

He now had responsibility for the government and the defence of the island, and it was not to be supposed, at first, that he would be left in peaceful possession of it. The threat of a counter-attack gradually receded, however, and he was free to respond to an appeal for help that came to him from Nelson early in 1799.

Nelson, now Rear-Admiral Lord Nelson of the Nile, had come under the sway of Emma Hamilton, wife of the British Minister at Naples, Sir William Hamilton, and Queen Caroline, consort of King Ferdinand. The French had invaded Naples, and Nelson had evacuated the royal family and the Hamiltons to Palermo, but Sicily appeared to be doomed unless help was forthcoming. It was a tactfully worded appeal that Nelson addressed to Charles, but the response to it was all that he could have hoped for.

Charles had no doubt that it would be in Britain's interests that Sicily should be prevented from falling into the hands of the French. He had no doubt, either, that he must act at once, if he was to act at all, and on his own authority. He sailed with as strong a force as could be spared, as soon as the necessary arrangements could be made, and he wasted no more time in Sicily.

The main force sailed for Messina, the loss of which would be likely to mean the loss of Sicily, but Charles disembarked at Palermo, and, having taken the precaution of obtaining full powers of command from Ferdinand, set out on horseback to survey the countryside, which might have to be fought over, and the coast, which would certainly have to be defended, if invasion came. Within weeks he had prepared a comprehensive plan for the defence of the island, and for guerrilla warfare in case defence failed, to the satisfaction of Nelson and Hamilton, and to the astonishment of Ferdinand and Caroline, who were accustomed to 'the greatest sloth in their method of transacting business', according to Charles himself.[16] Then, leaving Messina garrisoned, he returned to Minorca.

Later in that year, he was made a Knight of the Order of the Bath, but he was scornful of this mark of royal favour. He believed that the King had failed his father; and it rankled with him that the Duke of York should be given high military command because he was a Prince of the Blood, rather than because he deserved it. He may have been better pleased when he was made Governor of Minorca, soon afterwards.

His reputation as a soldier now stood high, and he found himself being consulted on military matters by both brother officers and members of the government. Pitt asked for his views on the future conduct of the war, and he produced for the Prime Minister what a military historian has called 'the first and only great strategic idea that had been put forward hitherto by any man, civil, naval or military'.[17] He pointed out that the French were over-extending their lines of communication in Italy, and he proposed that a strong force should be landed on the coast of Provence, close to the Italian border. What he was proposing, in effect, was an Italian peninsular war.

The recommendation was accepted by the Cabinet, and Charles, now Sir Charles, was put in charge of the operation, with a promise of twenty-thousand men. Three months later, however, when most of the preparations had been made, he was informed that he could have no more than five thousand men. At the same time, he was ordered to see that Malta, likely soon to be surrendered by the French, was returned to the Knights of St. John, its previous masters, who would be under the protection of the Tsar of Russia, and this was too much for him. It was his opinion that it would be foolish to hand over a valuable base to a potential enemy, and dishonourable to leave its inhabitants to the mercies of tyrants. He made his objections known, and then, in the spring of 1800, he resigned from his post.

A year later, at the age of forty-eight, he died, 'one of the great soldiers England has wasted'.[18] He was buried in St. Peter's Church, Petersham, near his home in Richmond Park, and a memorial to him was placed in Westminster Abbey.

LORD STUART DE ROTHESAY

IF THE STORY of the Stuarts of Highcliffe has a central character, it is Charles Stuart II, elder son of General Sir Charles Stuart and later Lord Stuart de Rothesay. He was born in 1779, and brought up at Bure Farm and the grace-and-favour residence in Richmond Park. He was at Eton from the age of eight to the age of sixteen, and he spent the next two years travelling in Europe, where and when the French Revolutionary War allowed, at first with his father and then alone. There followed a year at Oxford and a year at Glasgow University, and then more travelling, this time with his friend Henry Brougham, the future Lord Chancellor.

In 1800, while his father was making his abortive plans for an assault on the coast of Provence, he began, half-heartedly to read for the bar. When his father died, in the following year, he hoped to succeed him as M.P. for Poole, but the men of influence in the borough had other ideas. Soon afterwards, he was offered a post in the diplomatic service, and he accepted it without hesitation. Brougham remarked that 'nothing but absolute force ever kept him to the law'.[19]

Charles entered the diplomatic service at the time of the Treaty of Amiens, which brought the Revolutionary War to an end. But it soon became clear that Napoleon had no intention of resting on his laurels, whatever the French people might think, and Britain began to prepare for a resumption of hostilities. Shifting political circumstances had, by this time, brought the Knights of St. John within Napoleon's sphere of influence, more dangerous even than that of the Tsar, and it was decided that Malta should not, after all, be returned to them, but should be held as a British base. This may have been the correct decision, but it was a breach of the Treaty of Amiens and one of the causes of the First Napoleonic War, though for Charles it was a vindication of his father.

He was Secretary of Legation at Vienna 1801-1804, and Chargé d'Affaires during the Minister's absence 1803-1804. He was then Secretary of Embassy at St. Petersburg 1804-1808, and temporarily Minister Plenipotentiary 1806-1807, between the departure of one ambassador and the arrival of another. Napoleon's decisive victory at

Austerlitz, at the end of 1805, and the Tsar's meeting with Napoleon and change of sides at Tilsit, in 1807, were events of which he was a spectator from the sidelines.

In 1808, he was sent to French-occupied Spain on an unusual mission. He was to maintain channels of communication between Britain and the provincial juntas set up by Spanish patriots, and also to collect intelligence. But he interpreted his instructions freely, as he usually did, and constituted himself political adviser to the juntas until their success brought a free Spanish Government into being, when he was displaced by a British minister. He was expected to return to England, but he persuaded the Minister that he could still be useful in Spain.

A British army had arrived in Spain, by this time, with the object of joining forces with the Spanish and driving the French back into France, and its commander was General Sir John Moore, who, as Colonel Moore, had served with Charles' father in Corsica. Charles and General Moore were soon *en rapport*, and Charles was able to provide the General with valuable information and assistance. But the campaign was a disaster: the British army was forced to retreat to Corunna, where the troops were evacuated but Moore was killed; and the French regained their hold on the greater part of Spain.

From Spain, in 1809, Charles returned, briefly, to Vienna. And on this occasion it was a matter not of interpreting instructions freely but of acting with no instructions. Austria was sitting on the fence, and needed encouragement to come down on the British side, having been humiliated by the French too often in the past. Charles met the Austrian Foreign Minister, and then gave the British Foreign Secretary, George Canning, the benefit of his advice, but he was wasting his time. Official representatives of Britain and Austria had already agreed on what should be done; and though Austria came back into the war, she was soon knocked out of it again, by Napoleon, at Wagram.

Canning was not pleased with Charles' freelance diplomacy, and if he had remained Foreign Secretary he might not have been in a hurry to find him a new post. As it was, there had been a change of government, and the new Foreign Secretary was the Marquess Wellesley, an elder brother of the future Duke of Wellington - at this stage of his career the Viscount Wellington of Talavera, who was facing the French in Portugal with a fresh British army. The Marquess happened to have first-hand knowledge of recent events in Spain, and it is reasonable to suppose that he saw Charles as a man who could provide Wellington with diplomatic and political support. Be that as it may, in the new year of 1810 Charles was appointed British Minister at Lisbon.

Charles' position in Portugal was an uncomfortable one. A British army was fighting on Portuguese soil, and Portugal naturally wanted quick results; but the responsibility for obtaining results rested with Wellington, and he was not prepared to take unnecessary risks. At the same time, Portugal was receiving substantial amounts of aid from Britain, in the form of money and arms, and Wellington objected to the way in which it was being used. To complicate matters, the Prince Regent of Portugal had taken refuge from the French in the Portuguese colony of Brazil, and distance delayed any decision that was referred to him. As if that was not enough, there was often unhelpful criticism of Wellington - what he called 'croaking' - in British military and political circles.

Relationships, whether between individuals or nations, could not always be kept sweet, and conflicting interests could not always be reconciled, but Charles found ways and means of ensuring that Wellington was well served. He sometimes made himself unpopular, as when he threatened to withhold payments of financial aid unless the Portuguese authorities accepted certain recommendations concerning their management of the money,[20] but he was trusted and respected. He had the distinction of being made a member of the Portuguese Regency Council within a year of his arrival at Lisbon, and in 1812 the Prince Regent of England made him a Knight of the Order of the Bath. Wellington had recommended him to Lord Castlereagh, who had replaced Wellesley as Foreign Secretary, as deserving of some honour, only to find that Castlereagh had already recommended him to the Regent.[21]

The opposing armies swayed backwards and forwards across the peninsula until, at last, in 1813, Wellington was able to drive the French out of Portugal and Spain and back into France. Later in the same year, Britain's allies, emboldened by Wellington's successes, faced up to the French and beat them at Leipzig. In 1814, the armies of the allies converged on Paris, and the capital was surrendered to them. Napoleon abdicated and the war was over.

Sir Charles, as he now was, made sure that he was in Paris for the victory celebrations, and he persuaded Castlereagh to let him stay there as caretaker British Minister until Wellington, now Field Marshal the

Lord Stuart de Rothesay
by Baron Gérard
Victoria and Albert Museum Picture Library

Duke of Wellington, became Ambassador. His duties were not onerous, and when they were over he had only himself to please. He had the entrée to the Court of Louis XVIII, and Paris was full of foreign potentates and other distinguished visitors, but nobody interested him more than the ex-Empress Josephine, who held court with her family at Malmaison. 'I like Josephine better than anyone I have seen here,' he wrote to his mother, 'and I think all her family delightful.'(22)

He achieved the rank of ambassador at the beginning of 1815, when he was appointed to the Court of the Sovereign Prince of the Netherlands, that is Holland. Shortly afterwards, Belgium was united with Holland to form a new Kingdom of the Netherlands, with the Sovereign Prince as its King. At the same time, Napoleon returned to France, from exile on the island of Elba, and Louise XVIII fled across the border into exile at Ghent. Sir Charles was now accredited to the Court of the King of the Netherlands and, also, to the Court of the King of France in exile.

The Second Napoleonic War was fought in Belgium, and Sir Charles found himself working with Wellington again. It was a phoney war at first, and Brussels was *en fête* as the English colony made the most of the presence of the great Duke. Nobody believed that the final reckoning with Napoleon could be delayed for long, but the merry-making was still going on, at the Duchess of Richmond's Ball, when the alarm sounded.

The Duchess of Richmond's Ball, 'the most famous ball in history',(23) might not have been such a glittering occasion without Sir Charles. He lent the Duchess one of his attachés to help make the arrangements, and, on the night, he lent her his servants, in splendid liveries, and his silver plate.(24)

Wellington and Sir Charles both arrived at the ball aware of the fact that Napoleon had invaded Belgium, but determined not to do anything to encourage panic or spoil the party. Wellington had made his dispositions, and he could do no more until he had further intelligence. During the evening, he was brought the news that the French were moving fast towards Brussels, instead of skirting the city and attempting to cut him off from the sea, as he expected; at which he announced that it was time for him to go to bed. And he did go to bed, for two hours, once he had re-assessed the military situation and issued fresh orders.

In this emergency, Sir Charles was instructed to hand over the Netherlands embassy to a colleague and look to the safety of Louis XVIII, but it was not to be expected that he would be content to kick his heels at

Ghent, and he was in Brussels on that fateful day, 18th June, 1815, when Wellington and Napoleon met ten miles away at Waterloo. 'It has been a damned nice thing - the nearest run thing you ever saw in your life,' the Duke said to Thomas Creevey, several times over, after the battle.[25]

Having been given no contrary instructions since being told that he was to attach himself to Louis XVIII, Sir Charles accompanied the King on his return journey to Paris; and there he remained, uneasily, as ambassador *de facto* until he was acknowledged by the Foreign Office as ambassador *de jure*. Since he was there, he was told, he might as well stay there.[26] It was a time of change for him, and not only in that he was now Ambassador at Paris, 'the most desirable post in the Diplomatic Service', according to Canning, later.[27] The world that he knew was at peace for the first time since his childhood, and he was about to be married.

In 1816, when he was thirty-six and she was twenty-six, he married Lady Elizabeth Yorke, daughter of Philip Yorke, 3rd Earl of Hardwicke, a former Lord Lieutenant of Ireland and the grandson of the great Lord Chancellor. It was said to be a marriage of convenience, and perhaps it was more than a coincidence that Lady Elizabeth's background and accomplishments were those most likely to make her a successful ambassador's wife, but the relationship was based on respect and affection if it was not based on love. There were two daughters, in due course, Charlotte and Louisa, but no son, to Sir Charles' great disappointment.

The work of a British representative in France in the aftermath of the Napoleonic Wars was not easy, since even those French men and women who welcomed the return of Louis XVIII - perhaps chiefly those who had been loyal to the Bourbons during the Empire - resented the humiliations that the downfall of Napoleon had brought on their country; but Sir Charles did not suffer from lack of confidence. Castlereagh and Wellington were both in Paris for some time at this stage of affairs, looked to for as long as they were there as Britain's chief representatives, and this did not suit him at all.

When a new order of things was established, however, or when the old order of things was re-established, Sir Charles came into his own. The embassy building, the Hôtel de Charôst, was previously the home of Napoleon's sister Princess Pauline Borghese, which he, himself, had bought on behalf of the British Government, when he was caretaker

Minister at the end of the First Napoleonic War. It was a grand house; and here he and Lady Elizabeth lived and entertained in the grand style. But his social life was not by any means all frivolity: it kept the British flag flying; and it gave him the means of making informal contacts, collecting information to be passed on to the Foreign Office, and transacting political business off the record.

His unofficial duties were as important as his official duties, and intelligence gathering was particularly important, to judge from the recurrence of references to it in his papers, and to judge, too, from the amount spent on it in relation to the total cost of the Diplomatic Service.[28] It was his official duty to represent to the French Government the British Government's views on matters of moment, and of these, to judge again from his papers, the abolition of the slave trade was one that was particularly pressing in England. Unfortunately, it was not a popular cause in France.

There were many subjects on which the two governments failed to agree completely, such as the slave trade, but there were few that threatened diplomatic relations between them. A crisis arose in 1823, however, over France's support of King Ferdinand of Spain, in his defiance of the reasonable demands of his own people. Britain objected strongly, through Sir Charles, but France persisted, to the extent of sending an army into Spain. Sir Charles had then to deliver an ultimatum, which, having been delivered, was made public: Britain would not tolerate an occupation of Spain, any interference with the Spanish colonies or any incursion into Portugal. The Spanish colonies were an important market for Britain, and Portugal was Britain's oldest ally. Whatever effect Britain's stand may have had on France, the crisis passed, and ruffled feathers on both sides were smoothed.

Paris in those days was a centre of attraction for rich collectors interested in furniture and the decorative arts. Prominent among them were the Prince Regent and his friend the Earl of Yarmouth, later Marquess of Hertford, one of the founders of the Wallace Collection. Sir Charles was not a rich man, and he was not a collector in the strict sense of the word, but he was interested and he was a buyer, sometimes on behalf of others and sometimes on his own account. Canova's statue of Napoleon, which was presented to Wellington by the Regent and can be seen at Aspley House, was purchased by the Government through Sir Charles.[29]

If he was not a collector of any other sort, he was a bibliophile; and there is no doubt that he had been more than ordinarily interested in books since his schooldays. His account of his travels between leaving Eton and going up to Oxford is scattered with references to old libraries visited and incunabula examined.[30] And in the years that he spent in Paris he built up his own collection of books and manuscripts. His taste was both catholic and scholarly, and the range of his interests was the wider for the fact that he was an accomplished linguist. It was a huge collection. The library and the ante-library at Highcliffe, which were built for it, together make up the biggest room in the house, and, according to one estimate, 30,000 volumes could have been accommodated on the shelves.[31]

He was an enthusiastic patron of the theatre while he was in Paris, and he knew the great actors and actresses of the day, Talma and Mademoiselle George and others. It was said that he was more intimately acquainted than he should have been with some of the lesser lights of the stage. He certainly acquired the reputation of a womaniser, but he was not exceptional in this respect: few of his peers were known for their chastity.

George III died and was succeeded by the Prince Regent as George IV in 1820. This might have meant a change of government at home, with consequent changes in embassies abroad, but the new King kept his father's ministers, and Sir Charles was left in peace. Castlereagh committed suicide, in a state of depression, in 1822, and the Foreign Office reverted to Canning, who was no friend of Sir Charles. Even then, Sir Charles was left where he was, only disturbed by a hint from Canning that he would be replaced at an appropriate juncture. The death of Louis XVIII in 1824 was the occasion that Canning chose, and Sir Charles and his family returned to England at the end of that year.

Sir Charles' relationship with Canning, already poor, deteriorated when he complained about his recall and asked for a peerage. And he made matters worse when, in response to soundings by the East India Company, he said he would be prepared to accept the Governorship of Madras if he were assured of the Governorship-General of India in due course. Canning was outraged by this presumption, but he was saved from the Foreign Secretary's displeasure again, this time by the unaccountable intervention of the King.[32] Then he had another piece of luck: a diplomatic mission was planned, for which he had the qualifications most needed.

It was Canning's policy to foster friendly relations between Britain and the old Spanish colonies of South America. This was a matter of political and commercial commonsense to him, though it provoked much controversy, and he, himself, recognised the risk it involved of antagonising Spain and her supporters in Europe. When it came to extending the policy to the Portuguese colony of Brazil, his freedom of action was limited by the close ties that bound Britain and Portugal, and his solution to this problem was mediation. If Britain could help Portugal and Brazil to arrange a separation on amicable terms, he reasoned, she would gain the goodwill of both parties. Sir Charles, a senior and experienced diplomat, whatever his faults, was already known and trusted by the Portuguese, and he was acceptable to all concerned as mediator.

And so, in 1825, Sir Charles was appointed Ambassador on a Special Mission to Portugal and Brazil, and his dignity as such was supported by the provision of a 74-gun ship-of-the-line for himself and his suite. The mission was also a voyage of discovery for him, however, and he added to his party a physician, who was to double as botanist and zoologist, and an artist, Charles Landseer, brother of Edwin Landseer. It was recorded in his dispatches and letters, and also in Landseer's drawings, which were later published.[33]

In Portugal, he conferred with King John VI, who had been Prince Regent and had ruled from the safety of Rio de Janeiro during the Peninsular War, with the Foreign Minister and also with old friends from his days as British Minister at Lisbon, among them a certain countess, who is said to have been the unofficial source of much helpful information;[34] and he was given the powers of a Portuguese plenipotentiary. In Brazil, he had to deal with John VI's son Dom Pedro, whom John had left at Rio as his Viceroy and the Brazilians had declared Emperor.

Unfortunately, Dom Pedro and his ministers had already received overtures from a representative of the French Government, suggesting that France should recognise Brazil's independence, in return for certain commercial privileges, without the necessity for bringing Portugal into the matter. Sir Charles' first task, therefore, was to put the Frenchman in his place; and this he did by calling on him and reminding him that the Restoration of the Bourbons to the throne of France had depended on the

23

Highcliffe Castle, 1951
Aerofilms of Borehamwood

principle of legitimacy, making it clear that, in his view, the same principle should govern their dealings with Dom Pedro.

Thereafter, his negotiations proceeded smoothly, and the treaty by which Portugal recognised Brazil's independence was signed by him and the other plenipotentiaries less than six weeks after his arrival in Brazil, though another three months elapsed before the process of ratification was completed. There were celebrations in Lisbon and Rio, and Sir Charles was made Count of Machico, in Madeira.

But in London the celebrations were muted, and Sir Charles' success was overshadowed by failures, for which he was by no means entirely responsible. He had been instructed to take appropriate steps to safeguard Britain's trade with an independent Brazil; and he knew that his Government was working for the abolition of the slave trade, of which Brazil was the centre. Communications between Sir Charles and the Foreign Office, across the Atlantic, were such that proper consultations were impossible, so that he was often obliged to act on his own judgement; and, taking the opportunities that presented themselves to him, he concluded both a commercial treaty and a treaty to abolish the slave trade.

Canning was not satisfied with these two treaties, and though, at first, he was prepared to allow Sir Charles to re-negotiate them, he rejected them completely, later, when they were published in Rio as if they had been ratified by Britain as they were. Canning was angry at what he saw as a blatant attempt at manipulation, and Sir Charles was angry at what he saw as a reflection on him. New treaties were successfully negotiated, by others, not long afterwards.

When Sir Charles and his diplomatic colleagues were free, for the time being, of conferences and negotiations, they joined the other members of their party, who were exploring the country, collecting botanical and zoological specimens and making drawings of what they saw. One of the zoological specimens, a grey parrot, was sent home to his mother. He visited Bahia, but the ancient capital had flourished on the slave trade, and he was not welcome there. When there was no more that he could do about his treaties, he accepted an invitation from the captain of a British frigate to cruise with him along the coast.

Then a cat was let loose among the political and diplomatic pigeons, by the death of John VI and the accession of Dom Pedro to the throne of Portugal. Dom Pedro renounced the throne in favour of his eight year old daughter, Donna Maria, whom he proposed should be married to his younger brother, Dom Miguel; but, before his abdication took effect, he presented Portugal with a constitution that was bound to be seen, in many quarters, as dangerously democratic.

Sir Charles became involved in the situation thus created when Dom Pedro persuaded him to deliver the constitutional documents to the Regent whom he had appointed for Donna Maria, his sister, the Infanta Isabella, at Lisbon, having pointed out to him that he was still both a British and a Portuguese diplomat. Those who were suspicious of the constitution could only see his involvement as interference by Britain in Portuguese affairs, and Canning was worried. There was worse to come, but first Sir Charles received the thanks of the now legitimately styled Emperor Pedro I and was made Marquess of Angra, in Brazil.

Canning sent Sir Charles strict instructions to do nothing that could be construed as incompatible with his British diplomatic status while he was in Portugal, and to return to England as soon as his duty to Dom Pedro was done. But the Infanta Isabella, who was undoubtedly in need of advice, chose to treat him as her confidential adviser, and he responded to her in that character. He had interpreted instructions freely and acted without instructions before, but now he ignored them.

When he did return to England, towards the end of 1826, he was given a frosty reception at the Foreign Office. Not only had he disobeyed the Foreign Secretary's orders in Portugal, he had also written a series of arrogant and offensive letters to one of the under-secretaries during the course of the Special Mission, and he could not have expected rewards or thanks. His insubordination had, indeed, for the time being, cost him the English peerage on which he had set his heart.[35]

At the end of 1826, Canning, himself, had to take action in Portugal. Dom Miguel, a reactionary and unscrupulous man, did not wish to marry Donna Maria, but he was determined to have the throne for himself. He had the support of disaffected elements of the Portuguese Army and of supposedly irregular forces from Spain and France, two countries in which constitutions and democratic ideas were as dangerous infections. Unfortunately for him, however, the involvement of Spanish and French forces allowed the Portuguese Government to claim that the country was being attacked from outside its borders, and so to invoke its defence treaty with Britain. British soldiers were sent to Portugal, and among them was Sir Charles' nephew, Charles Stuart III.

Canning became Prime Minister at the beginning of 1827 but died four months later, to be succeeded by Frederick Robinson, newly created Viscount Goderich, who happened to be related to the Stuarts and the Yorkes. Goderich had been in office only a little longer than Canning when he resigned, to be succeeded by Wellington. It was Wellington who finally obtained a peerage for Sir Charles, though it was Goderich who first recommended it.

Sir Charles was created Baron Stuart de Rothesay of the Isle of Bute in the New Year of 1828. He was mentioned as a possible Foreign Secretary under both Goderich and Wellington.[36&37] But, in the summer of that year, to his great satisfaction, he was re-appointed Ambassador at Paris.

The Earl of Aberdeen became Foreign Secretary under Wellington, but there were certain aspects of foreign policy in which the Duke took a personal interest, one of these being relations between Britain and Portugal. Dom Miguel had managed, by devious means, to place himself on the throne of Portugal, and the various factions opposed to him called for the use of the British troops in the country to assist in removing him, but Britain had no treaty obligation and no inclination to intervene in a civil war. Wellington had had enough of war in the Peninsula, and his response to this development was to bring the troops home.

Lord Stuart de Rothesay's second term as Ambassador at Paris was dominated by the Revolution of 1830. Other matters claimed his attention in 1828 and 1829, however, among them serious differences in foreign policy between Britain and France, the death of George IV and the accession of William IV, and the exposure of a smuggling racket, involving the use of the diplomatic bag, which was widely believed to have been operated with his connivance.

The Revolution of 1830 was not a surprise to the *corps diplomatique*. Charles X, who had succeeded Louis XVIII, had attempted to put the clock back, and to rule as his forebears had ruled, in spite of the Revolution of 1789 and the fate of Louis XVI. In 1829, he dismissed his ministers because they were not sufficiently pliant, and appointed others in their places; and when, in 1830, there were elections, and the electorate, such as it was, expressed its disapproval of what he had done in unmistakable terms, he issued a set of decrees, the purpose of which was to render the results null and void and preserve the status quo.

Protests were dealt with in such a heavy-handed manner that they rapidly grew more dangerous and difficult to control. Scattered demonstrations developed into organised and co-ordinated attacks on public buildings. The army was called out, but the sympathies of many of the soldiers lay with the insurgents. The King was advised to make some conciliatory guesture, but he did nothing until it was too late to do anything; and then, when the mob had taken control of Paris and was about to turn its attention to him and his family, he abdicated.

Lord Stuart de Rothesay acted perfectly properly at first. He stayed at his post, having sent his wife and children out of Paris, and did his best to keep his Government in touch with the rapidly changing situation round him. He was loyal to Charles X, and, publicly at least, he held aloof from the several factions that were vying for power. But, already too inclined towards policies of his own making, he was now influenced by a romantic notion of the loyalty due to Charles when he was no longer king, and by a belief in the principle of legitimacy that made no allowance for political expediency; and he soon found himself sailing closer than ever before to the wind of professional disaster.

Charles X had abdicated in favour of his grandson, the Duc de Bordeaux, whose father, the Duc de Berri, had been assassinated in 1820. Before the royal party, which included the Duchesse de Berri and the Duc de Bordeaux, set off for one of the Channel ports and exile, Charles sent a message to Lord Stuart asking to be warned if any threat to the legitimate succession should arise. A threat soon did arise, in the form of the decision of those who held power in France to offer the throne to Louis Philippe, Duc d'Orléans, and Stuart dispatched one of his staff with this news to Charles, who had not yet left the country.

If Lord Stuart had confined himself to a statement of the facts he could not have been criticised, but he did not do so. He advised Charles to leave the Duc de Bordeaux in France, for the sake of the legitimist cause. Furthermore, he interpreted an offer that Louis Philippe had made immediately after the abdication, to take responsibility for the Duc de Bordeaux, as his endorsement of the scheme, regardless of the fact that circumstances had changed in the meanwhile.

The Duc de Bordeaux was not left in France, and Louis Philippe became King of the French. Lord Stuart's indiscretion did not become public knowledge, and no harm was done. But when Wellington heard the story from Lord Aberdeen, he was as angry with Stuart as Canning had ever been. He pointed out to Aberdeen that the presence of the Duc de Bordeaux in France, and the support that his presence gained for the legitimist cause, could have led to civil war, in which Stuart's intervention would have implicated Britain.[38] He saw Stuart's use of Louis Philippe's name as particularly dangerous, suggesting duplicity on the part of the new King of the French.

Wellington resigned at the end of 1830. Earl Grey became Prime Minister, and changes were made in Britain's representation abroad. Lord Stuart was replaced as Ambassador at Paris, and he and his family returned to England again at the beginning of 1831.

Lord Stuart returned to a London home in the newly built Carlton House Terrace, but he had always intended to build a country house for himself where his grandfather, Lord Bute, had lived at Christchurch, and now he was able to do so. He had already bought back part of the land that had belonged to Lord Bute and had been sold by his father, and he had also collected large quantities of stone and other building materials, much of it from the sites of ancient buildings in the north of France and some of it - most famously an oriel window - in the form of complete architectural features of these buildings.

The house was Highcliffe, now called Highcliffe Castle, a rare surviving example of the Romantic and Picturesque style of architecture. Lord Stuart's architect was William John Donthorn, a pupil of Sir Jeffry Wyatville, or Jeffry Wyatt, as he was at the time. Donthorn found Stuart a difficult man to please, and that is one of the reasons why the work, begun in 1831, was not completed until the end of 1834 or the beginning of 1835. Another reason was Lady Stuart de Rothesay's opposition to the project, on grounds of design and expense.

Books and manuscripts had pride of place in the house, in the enormous library that was designed for the collection, but everything in it had been chosen with care, as, over the years, opportunities to acquire what he would need for his future home, or simply appealed to his taste, had presented themselves. Highcliffe was a home for Lord Stuart and his family, and a showcase for furniture and furnishings, paintings, drawings and prints, sculpture and *objets d'art*, some of which can now be seen in the Victoria and Albert Museum.*

* The Bettine, Lady Abingdon Collection

A third reason for the delay in the completion of Highcliffe was that the country was in the grip of a political crisis. Lord Grey and the Whigs, in power, were commited to parliamentary reform, and Wellington and the Tories, in opposition, were determined to prevent it. Lord Stuart was a Tory, and he was active in his support for Wellington, though he seldom spoke in the House of Lords.

The Whigs had a majority in the House of Commons, but the Tories had a majority in the House of Lords, and the Lords were able to defy the Commons. When the stalemate seemed likely to provoke a social upheaval in the country, and Grey was pressing for the creation of enough Whig peers to outvote the Tories, Wellington bowed to pressure from the King, and let it be known that he would withdraw from the fray. The Duke's supporters, including Lord Stuart, followed suit, and the great Reform Bill was passed in 1832.

In 1834, Wellington was installed as Chancellor of the University of Oxford. The proceedings, part formal and part festive, lasted three days, and Oxford was full of the Duke's friends, among whom Lord Stuart was able to count himself. They had been close for many years by this time, in peace and in war, and the contretemps of 1830 had not come between them for long. Honorary degrees were conferred, and Stuart was made a Doctor of Civil Law.

He was without an appointment for ten years, and he was restless, even at Highcliffe. He travelled, sometimes with his family and sometimes alone, and his family became used to his comings and goings, surprising as they could be. On one occasion, he disappeared from a party at a country house, which - he later explained - had bored him, and was next heard of in Iceland.[39]

His last appointment was to St. Petersburg, as Ambassador, in 1841, when Victoria had been on the throne for four years, Sir Robert Peel was Prime Minister and Aberdeen was Foreign Secretary again. Unfortunately, his health broke down almost at once and he was soon unable to work, but he did not wish to have to resign and Aberdeen did not wish to have to remove him. Eventually, however, a way round the problem was found, and he was brought home.

He died at Highcliffe in 1845. He had built a church near the house, now the Parish Church of St. Mark, and it was there that he was buried.

CAPTAIN JOHN STUART R.N.

JOHN STUART, younger son of General Sir Charles Stuart, was born in 1780.[40] He was only eighteen months younger than his brother, Charles, but the two boys did not share much of their childhood. Charles was sent to Eton when he was eight, and John went to sea in 1794, a few months before his fourteenth birthday. He was not at Eton, but he may have been at Winchester, as his father is said to have been, since a boy called Stewart (sic) was there from 1791 to 1793.[41] The spelling of the name does not rule him out: it varies, in known references to him and other members of his family, from time to time in different records, and from place to place in the same records.

At that time, most potential officers entered the Royal Navy as *protégés* of a captain, without any reference to the Admiralty. Before 1794 they usually did so in the guise of servants, to whom captains and officers of certain other ranks were entitled, but it was in that year that the rating of officer's servant was abolished and replaced by the rating of volunteer, and aspirant officers were then known as volunteers of the first class. The minimum age for officers' servants and volunteers was thirteen, and the young gentlemen must have served at least six years at sea before they could apply for a commission as lieutenant. Two of the necessary six years of service at sea must have been spent in the rating of midshipman, and two years of service was one of the qualifications for that rating. These were the rules, but they were sometimes more honoured in the breach than the observance.

There are three main sources of information about John's career: the certificate of service supplied to support his application for a commission as lieutenant in 1800;[42] Steel's Navy Lists; and a few family letters, published and unpublished.[43&44] The first of these lists the ships in which he served and the length of his period of service in each, with his rating in each, between 1794 and 1800. The second contains monthly summaries of the movements of ships and senior officers, through which his changes of command, from 1802 onwards, can be traced. And the third supplies some information missing from the other two, such as his movements as lieutenant between 1800 and 1802.

He first went to sea rated captain's servant in the *Hornet*, 16 guns, and the Captain of the *Hornet,* in the rank of commander, was a certain Christmas Paul. Thereafter, for reasons that can only be guessed at, his rating varied. He was soon rated midshipman, in spite of the rules, and soon after that he was rated able-seaman. There is a gap in his recorded service at the beginning of 1795, perhaps to be accounted for by the fact that Paul was promoted and given another command, and a new captain was appointed to the *Hornet*. As midshipman again, he served under Captain Sir Charles Knowles, Bart, in the *Edgar*, 74 guns, and the *Goliath*, 74 guns, and then in the *Amphitrite*, 28 guns, under Captain Charles Herbert.

In 1797, he was transferred from the *Amphitrite* to *La Pomone*, 44 guns, commanded by Commodore Sir John Borlase Warren, under whom he continued to serve, with one brief interlude, until he was made lieutenant. There had evidently been trouble of some sort in the *Amphitrite*, and he had written to his parents about this and about his transfer. 'I received John's letter,' his father wrote to his mother, from Portugal, 'and upon the whole I am more happy now that he is with Sir John Warren.'[45] John was to tell Charles, later, that he was 'under the greatest obligation to Sir John'.[46] In the *Pomone*, however, he was rated first able-seaman and then volunteer. Later in the same year, when Warren was transferred, he was taken with the Commodore into the *Canada*, 74 guns, in which he was rated able-seaman and then midshipman.

His daily life had a fixed routine, but this was sometimes interrupted. In 1798, a squadron under Warren's command played a part in the suppression of the Irish Rebellion, and the frustration of attempts made by France to take advantage of it. The main rebel forces had been defeated, in two separate actions, and a French force sent to support them had arrived too late and had had to surrender. A second French force, accompanied by the rebel leader Wolfe Tone, then sailed for Ireland, cocking a snook at the British blockade as it slipped out of Brest.

Warren, forewarned, intercepted this expedition off the coast of Donegal. His was the superior force, an 80-gun ship, the *Foudroyant*, two 74-gun ships, one of them the *Canada*, and five frigates, compared with one 74-gun ship, the *Hoche*, and eight frigates; and only poor weather favoured the French. The *Hoche* and three frigates were captured at the time, and three more frigates were accounted for later. John was 'at Sir John's elbow' throughout the action,[47] though the *Canada* was not closely engaged.

The interlude in John's service under Warren came in 1799, when Warren was promoted rear-admiral and given a new appointment, and John was transferred to the *Naiad*, 38 guns, under Captain Michael de Courcy, rated able-seaman. Then he was transferred to Warren's flag-ship, the *Temeraire*, 98 guns, commanded by Captain Thomas Eyton, rated midshipman, and the Admiral's hand can be seen in this move. When Warren shifted his flag to the *Renown*, 74 guns, later that year, both Eyton and John went, too, and it was from the *Renown* that John took and passed the examination for lieutenant. The rules were observed, and he had been just six years at sea.

Not every young gentleman who passed the examination was made lieutenant straightaway, but there was no delay in John's case. Warren's influence can be detected again, though his may not have been the only patronage on which John could hope to be able to rely. His movements in the next twelve months are not well documented, but in 1801, the year of his father's death, he took part in the abortive attack on Boulogne mounted by General Stuart's old comrade-in-arms Lord Nelson.

Napoleon was known to be preparing to invade England, and Nelson was put in charge of counter-measures. He planned a pre-emptive strike, intending to destroy the shipping being assembled at Boulogne to ferry a French army across the Channel, and he chose to hoist his flag in the ship in which John was serving, the *Medusa*, 44 guns. When the time came, the *Medusa* and the other ships of Nelson's squadron stayed out at sea, while their boats carried boarding-parties into the harbour under cover of night; but the attack had been anticipated, and it was bloodily repulsed. John joined one of the boarding parties, and he was fortunate to survive the carnage, the more so as his sword was broken in his hand. The remains of the sword can be seen in the Royal Naval Museum at Portsmouth.

In spite of this fiasco, Napoleon did not attempt to invade England, and in the following year, 1802, the Treaty of Amiens brought the Revolutionary War to an end. John was promoted commander, and for the duration of the Peace of Amiens, a little over a year, he was Captain of the sloop *Termagant*, 18 guns, in the Mediterranean.

The *Termagant* carried official dispatches and official persons about the Mediterranean, particularly between Naples or Palermo and Malta. It was unexciting work, but there were unofficial diversions at sea and visits on shore. On one occasion, John took on board, as passengers, a certain prince and princess. 'I was in clover,' he confided in Charles. 'The princess', he said, 'was an extraordinarily handsome, agreeable French woman,' and 'the pleasantest companion in the world'.[48] On another occasion, he climbed Vesuvius and viewed the crater, at that time 'devoid of fire or anything hurtful'.[49]

Whether officially or unofficially, a certain amount of intelligence gathering was also done by the *Termagant*. Some of this intelligence was of a gossipy sort, fit to be passed on to Charles in letters that might be opened by anyone, but some of it was less innocent. There were, for instance, soundings taken in Spanish Mediterranean ports, in which the Admiralty showed a great interest.[50]

Britain declared war on France in the early summer of 1803, when it had become clear that to allow the Peace to continue would be to play into Napoleon's hands. At the same time, John was given command of the *Kent*, 74 guns, flag-ship of Rear-Admiral Sir Richard Bickerton, Commander-in-Chief in the Mediterranean, an important appointment, which, no doubt, he deserved. The fact is, however, that interest, in the sense of influence, which played a part in the careers of many, if not most, successful naval officers, played a part here. Lord St. Vincent, First Lord of the Admiralty, had recommended John to Bickerton, for his father's sake, six months earlier.[51]

As soon as war was declared, if not a little sooner, Bickerton's squadron took up its pre-arranged station, off Toulon, while other squadrons took up their stations off Brest and Rochefort. Napoleon's naval might was dispersed among these harbours, and Britain was safe as long as it could not be brought together to take control of the Channel. The defeat of Britain by military means depended on an invasion of England, and an invasion of England depended on control of the Channel. But, shortly afterwards, Bickerton was superseded by Nelson.

St. Vincent now intervened on John's behalf with Nelson, who can be assumed to have been well-disposed towards him already. 'I am most anxiously desirous that he should obtain the rank of post-captain,' he wrote,[52] and nothing could have been clearer than that. At the same time, Nelson evidently received from John's mother, Lady Stuart, the sort of letter that he was accustomed to receive from the friends and relations of young officers; and he replied to it kindly.

> Lord Nelson assures Lady Stuart that she may depend that he will be happy in paying attention to Captain Stuart, who he knows is a most excellent young man.[53]

And John was duly promoted post-captain, or full captain. He had been entitled to be addressed as captain in the rank of commander; having the rank made all the difference in the world. Promotion for post-captains was by seniority, and he could reasonably hope to become an admiral in due course.

Nelson had no intention of keeping the Toulon fleet out of action. Indeed, he wished to bring it to action and destroy it. He kept his main force out of sight of land, and did what he could to entice the French out into the open sea, but without success. He had no alternative but to watch and wait, interminably as it must have seemed, in all weathers, with no base nearer than Gibraltar or Malta, and no port elsewhere at which he could be sure of a friendly reception. Even Naples and the ports of Sicily had been closed to him, at the insistence of France. To make matters worse, economies introduced by the Admiralty during the Peace meant that he could not rely on being able to obtain supplies and replacements from England for some time, and then, in 1804, Spain came into the war on the side of France again. But Nelson was not fazed, and it was not the least of his achievements that he was able to maintain the health and morale of his men.

John shared the hardships and anxieties of those days. He was Captain of the *Kent* until the summer of 1804, when the ship was found to be unseaworthy, and he was ordered to take her to Malta for repairs. Admiral Bickerton, still in the Mediterranean though no longer Commander-in-Chief, then shifted his flag, and John with it, to the *Royal Sovereign*, 100 guns.

Early in 1805, the French Vice-Admiral Pierre de Villeneuve escaped from Toulon with his fleet. He was reported to have sailed south-east; and Nelson, commanding a squadron that included the *Royal Sovereign*, searched long and hard and increasingly desperately for him, finding Sardinia, Naples and Sicily safe and afraid that his destination

Captain John Stuart, R.N.
Miniature by an unknown artist
Royal Naval Museum, Portsmouth

must be Egypt. But a gale had spoiled Villeneuve's plan, whatever it had been, and driven him back to Toulon after only three days at sea.

Not long afterwards, Napoleon ordered his admirals to put to sea, come what might, rendezvous with their Spanish allies in the Caribbean and then, in the expectation that the Royal Navy would drop its guard at home to protect Britain's interests in the West Indies, double back in one great fleet to seize control of the Channel. This was not the master-plan for the invasion of England that Napoleon supposed that it was, but Villeneuve was able to keep to the first part of it, and he evaded Nelson's watchers outside Toulon so successfully that it was some time before they discovered in which direction he had sailed.

When Nelson set off into the Atlantic in pursuit of Villeneuve, Bickerton was left in command in the Mediterranean, but John was allowed to join the chase. He was given command of the *Swiftsure*, 74 guns, which had been built at Buckler's Hard, on the Beaulieu River, near Christchurch, and he was exultant. 'Only three years ago I arrived at Gib, lieutenant of the *Medusa* frigate', he wrote in one of his letters, 'and I sailed from there a few days since captain of a first-rate, to follow the fortunes of the gallant Nelson and his fleet, wherever they may be bound.'[54] It must have been a disappointment to him when, less than a month later, midway through the chase, he was transferred to *La Decade*, 36 guns, a frigate of which he was to be captain for the next four years.

Disappointment awaited them all in the West Indies. At Barbados, Nelson was told that a combined French and Spanish fleet had been sighted sailing south towards Trinidad. This fleet was actually at Martinique, to the north, and by the time Nelson realised that he had been misinformed Villeneuve, whose intelligence was more reliable, though less welcome, had deserted his friends and allies and sailed for Ferrol. Nelson sent the news to England and to Vice-Admiral Sir Robert Calder, who was keeping watch off Ferrol, and then he, himself, sailed for Gibraltar. From Gibraltar, he returned to England on leave.

John returned to Gibraltar via Lisbon, where he delivered dispatches from Nelson to the British minister. At Gibraltar, he heard that Calder had failed to prevent Villeneuve from reaching the safety of Ferrol. Then came the news that Villeneuve was at Cadiz, with a powerful combined fleet, watched over by a small naval force under Vice-Admiral Cuthbert Collingwood. Bickerton and Calder both made for Cadiz, to support Collingwood, with the *Decade* as one of Bickerton's squadron.

The concentration of enemy naval power, French and Spanish, at Cadiz was an ominous development; but, at the same time, it presented the Royal Navy with an opportunity to break that power once and for all. Nelson had been waiting for such an opportunity and, after hurried conferences at the Admiralty and emotional scenes at Merton, where he was living with the widowed Lady Hamilton, he left England for the last time. He sailed from Portsmouth in the *Victory* on 15th September, 1805.

Meanwhile, Bickerton had fallen ill, and John had been ordered to bring him home. The *Victory* and the *Decade* met at sea on 20th September, and John was able to reassure Nelson that he could still depend on finding the enemy fleet at Cadiz.[55] Nelson wrote to Collingwood:

> I fell in with *Decade*, on 20th, 27 leagues S.W. from Scilly. It blew then very strong at S.W. I saw Captain Stuart for a moment. Sir Richard was far from well.[56]

And John wrote to his mother:

> If you are at Bure I hope soon to embrace you, as I trust I may have two days leave before sailing. I met Lord Nelson three days ago at the entrance to the Channel, and received orders to put myself under his command, and after victualling and refitting at Portsmouth to join him off Cadiz.[57]

But John was not at Trafalgar on 21st October, when Villeneuve and the combined fleet finally faced Nelson. His orders had been countermanded, and the *Decade* had joined the Channel Fleet.

The nature of the war at sea changed after Trafalgar. Napoleon could no longer hope for naval supremacy, and so was obliged to shelve his schemes for an invasion of England, but he could still defeat Britain by economic means. Britain's economy depended on her trade, and her trade depended on safety at sea and access to foreign ports for her merchant shipping, both of which Napoleon planned to deny her. The Royal Navy could not enforce access to foreign ports, but it could protect merchant vessels from enemy warships and privateers, which were equally dangerous.

At the beginning of 1806, after the death of Pitt and the formation of the Ministry of All the Talents, St. Vincent was appointed Commander-in-Chief of the Channel Fleet for the second time, having been called out of retirement. John thus found himself serving under his patron in the last, extra, months of the old admiral's career. The *Decade* belonged to a squadron under the command of Rear-Admiral Sir Richard Strachan, which spent several months of that year detached from the fleet, with another squadron under the command of Sir John Warren, now Vice-Admiral, searching for two squadrons of the Brest fleet.

These two squadrons had set out to prey on British merchant shipping in the South Atlantic and the West Indies, and they had proved elusive. They were eventually accounted for. Though ships of Strachan's squadron were in action in the western Atlantic with ships of one of the French squadrons, the ships of both the British and the French formations had been scattered by a hurricane, and neither the *Decade* nor Strachan's flagship, the *Caesar*, was at the scene.

An outline of John's service in the years that followed, that is his movements in the *Decade* and his changes of command, when they came, can be traced through the Navy Lists, but details are rarely to be found in any of the available sources of information. Trade protection continued to be one of the Royal Navy's most important duties, and occasional notes in the Navy Lists show that he had his share of them. Against the *Decade*'s entry for the month of May 1807, for instance, is the note: 'Convoy to West Indies'. Even after Trafalgar, however, Napoleon did not entirely abandon the idea of an attack on England from Ireland, where he was assured of a welcome and support from a certain section of the population. Vigilance was necessary, and the *Decade* and others of John's ships are sometimes listed as being in Irish waters.

Later in the year 1807, when the *Decade* was temporarily out of commission at Portsmouth, John was married, by special licence, at Christchurch Priory, his family's parish church when they were at Bure. His bride was Albinia Sullivan, daughter of John Sullivan, a nabob and a member of the Indian Board of Control. Albinia's mother was Lady Henrietta, daughter of George Hobart, 3rd Earl of Buckinghamshire,[58] and Lady Henrietta's mother and John's mother were sisters,[59] so that John and Lady Henrietta were first cousins, an odd state of affairs, explained by the fact that there were twenty-two years between the ages of the sisters.[(60)] John and Albinia had one child, a son, Charles, who was born in 1810.

In 1807, too, France invaded Portugal from Spain, now not an ally but a vassal state. The Prince Regent of Portugal and the Portuguese fleet were whisked away at the last minute, and the Portuguese island of Madeira, important for its position on the route to the Cape of Good Hope and India, was placed under British rule. The *Decade* became a familiar sight at Madeira between 1807 and 1809.

In 1808, however, there were popular uprisings against France in Spain and Portugal. Britain was called on for her support, and the Peninsular War began, giving the Royal Navy new duties. British troops and their arms and equipment, arms and equipment for the Spanish and Portuguese forces and, last but not least, large amounts of specie, that is hard cash, had to be transported to the theatre of war, either in warships or in other vessels escorted by warships. And when the grandly and alliteratively named Loyal Lusitanian Legion was take to Oporto that summer, its maverick commander, best known later as General Sir Robert Wilson, sailed in the *Decade*.

The buccaneering Wilson was a lieutenant-colonel in the British Army, who had already acquired an Austrian knighthood and was about to acquire the Portuguese rank of brigadier-general. His force was made up chiefly of Portuguese soldiers who had escaped the French Army, come to England and set up camp together, to the embarrassment of the British Government and the Portuguese Ambassador in London. Wilson wanted a command, the patriots of Oporto needed military assistance and the Portuguese soldiers in England, who had outstayed their welcome, were waiting for an opportunity to strike a blow for their own country. The expedition suited everyone, and Wilson was pleased by everything about it. 'I sailed in the *Decade* with your brother John,' he wrote to Charles, now in Spain, 'and a more sensible good fellow I never met in my life.'[(61)]

John returned to Portugal twice, in 1810, first in the frigate *Clyde*, 38 guns, and then in the frigate *Saldhana*, 36 guns. It was a year in which the losses of British shipping to privateers was particularly heavy, and one of these predators was captured by the *Clyde* on her outward voyage.[(62)] It was also the year in which Charles was appointed British Minister at Lisbon, and during the *Clyde*'s visit the brothers spent some time together. 'I cannot let the packet sail without telling you that we are both well, living in a fine house, beautiful climate and situation and in good society,' Charles wrote to their mother, soon after John's arrival.[63] If they met during the *Saldhana*'s visit, it may have been for the last time.

He was in Irish waters again later in 1810, at a time when the British Government had particular reason to be on its guard against the activities of those partners in revolution, the Irish nationalists and the French, and it was in Lough Swilly in 1811 that he died, on board the *Saldhana*. He died on active service though not in action, and the cause of his death was probably one of the diseases that was endemic in the navies of those days, of which the most common, at least in temperate climates, was typhus.

He was buried in St. Peter's Church, Petersham, close to the grave of his father, whom, according to the composer of his epitaph, he resembled both in appearance and in character. Like his father, he had a stern sense of duty; whether or not he had the same qualities of leadership as General Stuart, the available records do not make clear.

He left his wife and his one year old son.

LADY CANNING

LORD STUART DE ROTHESAY had no son, but two daughters. Both were born at the British Embassy in Paris, Charlotte, known as Char, who became Viscountess and Countess Canning, in 1817, and Louisa, known as Lou, who became Marchioness of Waterford, in 1818.

When Charlotte and Louisa were seven and six, respectively, Lord Stuart de Rothesay, then still Sir Charles Stuart, was recalled from Paris, and they exchanged the Embassy for Wimpole Hall, near Cambridge, the home of their maternal grandparents, the Earl and Countess of Hardwicke, and - when it was ready for them - Bure Farm, later called Bure Cottage and Bure Homage*. The farmhouse, which had belonged to their paternal grandparents, General Sir Charles and Lady Stuart, was the only home that their father could then call his own; it was a simple building, and it was enlarged and refurbished for its new occupants.

Charlotte and Louisa remained in England, with Lady Elizabeth, their mother, when Sir Charles was sent to Portugal and Brazil, but the family returned to Paris together in 1828, when, as Lord Stuart de Rothesay, he was re-appointed Ambassador to France. The children were old enough, now, to assimilate something of French culture, and to perfect their knowledge of the French language. They were ready, too, to be introduced to the social life of the French capital.

A costume ball given by the Duchesse de Berri, at the Tuileries, in 1828, is mentioned in several of the memoirs of the period, as being the most spectacular of what Lady Jackson called that lively young widow's 'Court gaieties'.[64] The theme of the ball was the Court of Francis II and his Queen, Mary Stuart - Mary, Queen of Scots, Francis being represented by the young Duc de Chartres, eldest son of Louis Philippe, Duc d'Orléans, and Mary Stuart by the Duchesse de Berri, herself. Louisa appeared in the guise of a lady-in-waiting, and though Charlotte is not mentioned it is unlikely that she was left out. 'All the

---

*   Since demolished

youngest and most fashionable members of society were given a place in this company', according to the Comtesse de Boigne.[65]

When trouble was brewing in Paris in the summer of 1830, Lord Stuart de Rothesay sent his family away on a tour of the south of the country. Lady Stuart de Rothesay, Charlotte and Louisa, accompanied by the governess who had recently joined the family, travelled in a britzka - an open carriage with a folding hood, and their servants followed in a coach. They were at Pau when they heard the first news of the Revolution, and they witnessed there the unceremonious substitution of the tricolour for the white flag of the Bourbons above the prefecture. A few days later, they heard that Charles X had abdicated and Louis Philippe was King. They continued their tour, however, and soon after they arrived back at the Embassy, in the autumn, Lord Stuart's second term as Ambassador came to an end.

The Stuart de Rothesays' home in England was now Carlton House Terrace, in London. Bure Cottage had been sold and Highcliffe was not yet built, though a small house that was to be converted into an east wing for Highcliffe provided a temporary country retreat. In London, Lord Stuart de Rothesay was soon caught up in the drama of parliamentary reform; as a Tory, and as a friend and supporter of the Duke of Wellington, he was opposed to change. Lady Stuart de Rothesay, meanwhile, oblivious of the cataclysm that the Tories, by their obduracy, risked bringing on them all, made it her business to establish herself and her daughters on the English social scene. She had reason to be proud of Char and Lou: they were beautiful, a fact that was much remarked, if only because neither Lord Stuart nor Lady Stuart had the least claim to good looks; they were charming; and they were talented.

They were close as children and remained so, and they were alike in many ways. They were devoted to their parents and all their family, gentle and devout, but strong-minded, and, most obviously, artistic. Char was probably the more intelligent and the more appreciative of humour, but she was not Lou's equal as an artist.

When Char was eighteen, she fell in love, but by a strange irony the young man was Charles Canning, known as Carlo, son of Lord Stuart de Rothesay's *bête noir*, George Canning. Lord Stuart would not agree to an engagement at first, but he could not bring himself to stand in the way of his daughter's happiness for long; and he faced a powerful lobby of match-makers, inside and outside the family. Char and Carlo were married in 1835; and in 1837 the death of Carlo's mother, a peeress in her own right, made them Viscount and Viscountess Canning.

The early years of Char's marriage were filled with country-house visits and travel. She and Carlo had no home of their own until old Lady Canning died, when her house in Grosvenor Square came to them. Carlo was briefly an M.P., but his duties as such did not demand much of him, and his removal from the House of Commons to the House of Lords, at a time when his party was in opposition, left him without any desire to devote himself to politics. In 1838 and 1839, they made a long voyage in Carlo's yacht, and Lord Stuart de Rothesay went with them as far as Venice, which was *en fête* for a visit of the Emperor Ferdinand I of Austria. In 1840, they returned to the Mediterranean, and they left the yacht in the spring of 1841 to spend some time in Rome.

There was a change in the government in 1841, when Lord Melbourne and the Whigs were replaced by Sir Robert Peel and the Tories, with Lord Aberdeen as Foreign Secretary, and this had important consequences for Char and her family. Lord Stuart de Rothesay was appointed Ambassador to Russia, and Carlo was made Under-Secretary for Foreign Affairs. The following year brought an important change in Char's own life: it was in 1842 that she became a lady of the bedchamber to Queen Victoria.

Char served the Queen as a lady-in-waiting for thirteen years, in which time, as their journals and letters show, sovereign and subject came to know each other well. From the first, the Queen found Char 'a remarkably nice person, so quiet, unaffected and gentle and so ready to do anything';[66] later, she recognised other qualities in her, such as steadfastness and compassion. Char's letters to the Queen, particularly those written after she had left the Royal Household, expressed great respect and warm personal regard. The letters from India, always interesting and informative and often entertaining, gave Victoria a unique insight into the country's affairs, and she was grateful for this. 'She loved Your Majesty dearly', Carlo told the Queen when Char died.[67]

Queen Victoria expected her ladies to be able to draw and paint, and Char excelled in this respect. She had shown promise as a child, and she had lessons from W.L. Leitch, J.D. Harding and other artists. Watercolours of landscapes and buildings were her forte, and these were much in demand by the Queen as records of her travels. Such records of Char's own life in India, enlivened with the figures of men and women and various animals, include the best of her work, though John Ruskin much admired her flower paintings from India.[68]

Her drawings and paintings for Queen Victoria remain in the Royal Collection, at Windsor. Those that she did not give away, to the Queen or to her family and friends, found their way, eventually, through family connections, to Harewood House, in Yorkshire, the home of the Earls of Harewood. However, there are now examples of her work, which came from Highcliffe, at the Victoria and Albert Museum.[69]

One of the most memorable events of 1843 for the Queen's entourage, if not for the Queen herself, was the first foreign visit of the reign, to the French royal family, at the Château d'Eu in Normandy. The new royal steam-yacht, the *Victoria and Albert*, was used, and the party cruised along the south coast of England before crossing the Channel to Le Tréport. There was much pomp, but there was informality, too, and Char had many enquiries after her father from those who had known him when he was in France, Louis Philippe and Queen Marie-Amélie among them. The visit was counted a great success.

Lord Aberdeen accompanied the Queen, as Foreign Secretary, and also of the party was the Lord Steward of the Royal Household, Lord Liverpool. Char found Lord Liverpool a self-important man, and she was amused by a story that Lord Aberdeen had to tell her about him one morning, on board the *Victoria and Albert*. The Lord Steward had locked himself into his cabin, and had extricated himself eventually with the aid of pincers, lowered to his porthole on a piece of string. Recording this episode, in the journal that she was writing at the time in lieu of letters, Char averred that he had 'almost made up his mind to be drawn out thro' his port from the outside'. 'We all regret this was not done', she added.[70]

Other foreign visits followed. Soon after the Queen had returned to England from France, she set off again, with Char as one of her ladies, to Belgium, where a royal progress took her from Ostend to Bruges, Ghent, Brussels and Antwerp. Waterloo was not on her itinerary, for diplomatic reasons, but Lord Aberdeen rode out to the field from Brussels one day before breakfast, with the Duke of Wellington's younger son. This was a happy visit for Victoria, who was fond of King Leopold, her uncle. A visit to Germany two years later, however, which she had expected to enjoy, since her husband was to take her to meet his family and see his former home, was not a success. It seems that there was jealousy of Prince Albert in some quarters, and that he was not given the precedence as her consort that she thought proper everywhere, though Char had little to say about this.

The Queen and her family spent several holidays in Scotland before the Balmoral estate was acquired for Prince Albert in 1852, and Char was with them at Blair Castle in Perthshire, the home of Lord Glenlyon, in 1844. Her privacy and the relative simplicity of her life there appealed to the Queen, but the beauty of the place was its greatest attraction. Char was not the only artist to be employed at Blair Castle: Charles Landseer, who had been in Brazil with her father, and William Leitch, her teacher, were summoned; and the Queen, herself, put pencil and brush to paper.

Char's father died in 1845. He had been ill for several years, and his death was not unexpected. He spent the last days of his life at Highcliffe with Lady Stuart de Rothesay, and Char was with them at the end.

In waiting in London and at Windsor, Char played her part in the routine of royalty, as it was repeated with variations year by year, sometimes involving the full panoply of state, but sometimes dull and even tedious. For her, it might mean standing for hours behind the Queen's chair or, as on the day of the opening of the Royal Exchange, in 1844, driving to the City with the Queen in a gold coach, through cheering crowds.

When she was not in waiting and Carlo, too, was able to be away from London, country-house visits and travel would occupy them. Often, specially if Carlo could not be with her, she would spend the time with her mother at Highcliffe. At the end of 1846, Carlo found himself without government office, and they were able to spend several months in Rome; in 1852, in a new yacht, they sailed to Vigo, and went on by road to Santiago de Compostela, and then returned to cruise along the west coast of Scotland; and in Paris, in 1854, they were presented to the Emperor Napoleon III, who had come to power after Louis Philippe's downfall in the Revolution of 1848.

The Crimean War broke out in 1854, and Florence Nightingale went out to Scutari with her nurses. More nurses were soon needed, and Char was prominent among a group of people who took responsibility for finding them. There was no shortage of volunteers, but by no means all the would-be recruits were suited to the work that they would be expected to do. Some, for instance, seemed likely to ignore their patients' bodily ills

by Edward Ward
The Royal Collection © Her Majesty The Queen

in their zeal for the salvation of the men's souls. Char's job was selection, and her work in support of Florence Nightingale has been largely unsung.

Carlo had been brought back into government as Postmaster-General in 1853, by Lord Aberdeen, and he was confirmed in office and given a seat in the Cabinet in 1855, by Lord Palmerston, who replaced Aberdeen. It was later in 1855 that he was offered the Governorship-General of India, to his own surprise and that of the Queen, and he hesitated to accept this great prize perhaps only because it would be to turn his back on the prospect of a successful political career at home, now being held out to him by Palmerston. There may, however, have been personal matters to be considered.

The fact was that Char's marriage was no longer as happy as it had been at first, and it is said that Carlo was involved in a relationship with another woman, though surprisingly little is known about any such affair. It has been suggested, too, that powerful friends arranged for him to be offered the Governorship-General in order to detach him from the other woman,[71] but there is no good evidence that this was the case.[72] All the same, Char hinted at some private reason for going to India in spite of what she called 'one's own feelings and dislikes against it'.[73]

Whatever the truth of the matter, Carlo was duly appointed Governor-General; and he and Char arrived in Calcutta at the beginning of 1856. They were both immediately caught up in quasi-royal pomp and circumstance, to an extent that Char found oppressive, and, for all that, Carlo saw that his work would make him 'little better than a galley-slave'.[74] At first, Char was lonely: time hung heavily on her hands; she saw little of Carlo, and few in her circle could be counted as friends. There were frequent official engagements, but these were often to be endured rather than enjoyed; and even so private an unofficial engagement as going to church was taken over by protocol.

But if protocol was restricting, the heat of India was crushing and controlling. During what was admitted to be a particularly unpleasant spell of weather, soon after the Cannings' arrival, Char told a friend in England that the temperature in her room was 'very endurable' as long as all the doors and windows in the house were tightly closed and covered on the outside, but passing an open door or window was 'like passing the mouth of a foundry'. 'Any attempt to go out, even in a carriage,' she wrote, 'makes one gasp and dissolve immediately.'[75]

Then, almost without warning, in 1857, the Mutiny was upon them. It was the bloodiest incident in the history of British India, and it shook Britain's pride and confidence in herself to their foundations. Carlo was bitterly criticised for his management of the crisis until it was over, when his efforts could be seen in better perspective; but its causes could be traced back to the time of his predecessor, the Marquess of Dalhousie.

Lord Dalhousie's policies had been largely progressive and reforming, but he had moved too fast for some sections of Indian society, in which change was perceived as threat and religious susceptibilities were easily offended. One of his policies was to bring native states under British rule whenever it seemed possible or necessary to do so, and in most cases he acted when the native ruler died without a natural heir, regardless of the fact that adoptive heirs played an important part in the Hindu religion. He annexed the State of Oudh, however, because it was badly ruled, a move that seemed right and proper to him but not by any means so to the people of Oudh.

All might have been well, still, if the native soldiers of the Bengal Army had not become convinced that their British officers meant to foist on them the use of cartridge grease made from the fat of cows and pigs, which would have defiled both Hindus and Muslims. The men's fears, on this and other accounts, were unreasonable in several respects, and unnecessary in that the authorities concerned were willing to address them; but it was of the essence of the problem that the men no longer trusted the authorities. It was men recruited into the Bengal Army from Oudh who were the agents of the Mutiny, and, devastating as the outbreak was, it did not affect either of the other two Indian armies, or spread far from the upper reaches of the Ganges.

The men first turned on their officers at Meerut, not far from Delhi, and Delhi was theirs for the asking, since there were no British troops in the city. Then Lucknow and Cawnpore fell to them, though the Residency at Lucknow was successfully defended, and it was at Cawnpore that, in the worst of the atrocities committed on either side, British women and children were butchered in cold blood. Such acts of barbarity were counterbalanced, to some extent, by acts of great humanity; all the same, soldiers became inured to savagery, and civilians became used to siege conditions, fear, deprivation and disease.

In Calcutta, the Governor-General worked day and night to bring the situation under control. He was hampered by problems of manpower, logistics and communication, compounded by vast distances and burning heat, and harassed by a hostile press in England and India. The British Government failed to give him the support that he had a right to expect, but - to Char's satisfaction - the Queen repeatedly showed her confidence in him. Char, meanwhile, though anguished by the news that was shared with her day by day, and by what it meant to her husband, remained undaunted. She made it her business to support Carlo in whatever way she could, and to show her own confidence in him by keeping to the established pattern of her life, come what might. But she found it difficult, and all the more so for the fact that she was still unsure of Carlo's feelings for her.

There is a poignant reference to Char at this time in the account of the British rulers of India by one of Carlo's successors, the Marquis Curzon of Kedleston.[76] Lord Curzon wrote at length about Carlo and his term of office, and concluded that he covered himself with 'the vesture of real greatness' by the manner in which he met the challenge of the Mutiny. Then he turned to Char.

> By the side of Canning we see the gentle and tragic figure of his accomplished wife, her youth and beauty ebbing away under the appalling strain, her happiness, though not her devotion, shadowed by a cloud, the blame for which had been exclusively his, and for which after her premature death he felt endless remorse.

It was more than a year before the pacification of India was complete, and half-way through the process, at the beginning of 1858, Carlo moved to Allahabad, to be closer to the scenes of action. He would not allow his staff to take their wives with them, and so he could not allow Char to go either. There was some consolation for her in the fact that her cousin, Colonel Charles Stuart, had come out to India, with his wife, Minny, to be Military Secretary to the Governor-General, since Minny would be a companion for her. And there was another welcome addition to the household at the same time, a new A.D.C. called Johny Stanley, who amused Char and became devoted to her.

There was no reason why Char should stay in Calcutta without Carlo, and she spent the hottest months of that year, with Minny Stuart, accompanied by Johny Stanley and a second A.D.C., in the Nilgiri Hills, safe in the south of India. At every stage of the long journey - by sea to Madras, and then inland to Vellore, Bangalore, Mysore and Ootacamund - she was received as befitted the wife of the Governor-General, but at her destination, Coonor, south of Ootacamund, she was able to please herself and live relatively simply. She thrived in the cool and seclusion of the hills, and she spent the days walking and riding, often stopping to sketch or to collect flowers and plants; but Minny Stuart did not share her enthusiasms. Johny Stanley, writing to his mother from Coonor, said he enjoyed walking with Lady Canning - 'she walks like a goat while Mrs. S puffs and blows and requires lifting over stones 1 ft high'.[77]

Eventually, later that year, against his better judgement, Carlo was prevailed on to allow Char to join him at Allahabad. He did not believe it was yet safe for her to venture so far into the mutineers' country, but she was never in danger, on the journey or at Allahabad. Nothing she faced when they were physically together again, after seven months, was worse than the knowledge that they were as far apart as ever in an emotional sense. She kept her unhappiness to herself, however, as she had always done, and her letters were full of other things, such as Carlo's work and his health, the military mopping-up operations and the appropriation of the Government of India by the Queen.

The territories controlled by the East India Company had passed to the British Crown to all intents and purposes in 1833, and the Company had been merely the Crown's agent since then. Carlo had been nominated Governor-General by the Company's Court of Directors, and approved as such by the Crown in the form of the Board of Control. Now, in 1858, the Crown took over full responsibility for these territories, with those that had been added to them in the meanwhile, and the Governor-General became also Viceroy. A proclamation by the Queen, marking the occasion, was read simultaneously at ceremonies at Allahabad, Calcutta and elsewhere, and at Allahabad there were great celebrations.

At Calcutta again in the following year, 1859, there was more for the Cannings to celebrate. Peace was finally re-established throughout India, and Carlo was given a step in the peerage. He was now Earl Canning. More important to Char than Carlo's styles and titles, however, was their relationship, and it seems that it regained some of its old warmth in a quiet interlude that year at the Viceroy's country home at

Barrackpore, outside Calcutta. There was no holiday for Carlo, but at least, in those five weeks, he found time for himself and for her.

The Stuarts had sailed for England by this time, but they corresponded with Char regularly during the two years that were left to her. No doubt, too, they compared notes with her mother, Lady Stuart de Rothesay, at Highcliffe. Char was no less reticent than usual, but her family could read between the lines. 'I have much reason to think that the last two years have been happier to both than they had known for many, many passed ones', Minny Stuart wrote to a friend later.[78]

Towards the end of that year, the Viceroy and a vast and magnificent retinue began a progress through the north of India, from Calcutta to Cawnpore, Lucknow, Agra, Delhi, Ambala, Lahore and Peshawar. He wished to see certain parts of the country that he had not been able to visit before, including those that had been most affected by the Mutiny, and it was thought politic that he should show himself as widely as possible as the Queen's representative. A series of durbars was held, and at each the notables of the area were received in state. Char was delighted to be with Carlo, and pleased to see more of India, but she did not enjoy travelling hour after hour through heat and dust, or making a temporary home in a tent, however grand it might be, at the end of a tedious journey.

At Cawnpore, the horrors of the events that had taken place there were brought home to them by a tour of the dismal ruins of the place, with one of the few Englishmen who had lived to tell the tale. A church and a monument were planned as memorials to all those who were killed, and it was Char who produced the design that was used for the monument. Agra impressed them for altogether different reasons, and though Char admitted to having become bored by the accounts of the Taj Mahal to which she had been subjected, before and since she had come to India, she could not resist giving the Queen her own description of its beauty.

The progress brought them round from Peshawar to Simla, where, in the hills, Carlo and Char intended to spend the summer of 1860 together. To Char's intense disappointment, however, Carlo was summoned back to Calcutta soon after they had arrived, and he would not allow her to travel with him. The heat of the summer was at its worst, and the journey would be long and arduous.

Instead, it was agreed that the next stage of her journey towards Calcutta should be an expedition through the hills to Mussoorie. The distance between Simla and Mussoorie in a straight line was no more than seventy miles, but the way was circuitous and mountainous, and it took her as far into the Himalayas as India's border with Tibet. It was an extraordinary expedition for a woman to undertake at that time. Afterwards, she was surprised that it had been suggested to her, and said she certainly would not recommend it to her friends. But she did not in the least regret it, and she wrote a long account of it for the Queen.

This time, Char had been away from Calcutta for nearly a year, but soon, towards the end of 1860, she was off again with Carlo on another grand tour, less ambitious and with less about it that was harrowing than the first. They visited Patna, Benares, Maihar and Jubbulpore, and more durbars were held, two being held at Jubbulpore in order to obviate problems of precedence for certain of the Indian princes. One of the princes organised a tiger shoot in honour of the Viceroy, but no tiger appeared, and Carlo was hard put to it to remain viceregal. 'He found it a weary day sitting with the Rajah in a tree,' said Char, in a letter to the Queen.[79]

Most of her letters in 1861, the last year of her life, contained some reference to 'going home'. Carlo's term of office had been extended twice, but it was not to be extended again; and they were to leave India early in 1862. Her family in England had never been far from her thoughts, and the death of her grandmother, Lady Hardwicke, though she was an old lady, and more particularly the death of her brother-in-law, Lord Waterford, in a hunting accident, had grieved her. She longed to be with her mother and sister.

She had one ambition to satisfy before she left India, however, and that was to visit Darjeeling, a hill station in the Himalayas, like Simla and Mussoorie, but perhaps the most beautiful of them all, with the advantage of being the closest to Calcutta. Carlo had arranged to visit Allahabad, and it was agreed that she should go to Darjeeling and then on to join him, though he advised her later to go directly back to Calcutta. She was delighted with all that she saw of forests, hills and mountains, and though rain and mist interfered with some of her plans she was able, at dawn one day, to watch the first light reach Everest. It is said that letters passed between Char and Carlo every day while she was at Darjeeling. All that has survived of this correspondence is a few of Char's letters to Carlo, but these are fond and happy letters.

She was not completely well when she left Darjeeling, and she was seriously ill by the time she arrived at Calcutta. Carlo arrived from Allahabad shortly afterwards, and everything possible was done for her. There seemed to be reason for hope at first, but then her condition deteriorated rapidly, and she died in Carlo's arms.

She was buried at Barrackpore, and Carlo composed a moving epitaph. A more objective comment on her life and death, however, was made, much later, by one of Carlo's biographers.

> If to Canning himself the blow was a staggering one, probably abbreviating his life, the sense of loss was universal. Everywhere she had passed, Lady Canning had left a memory of charm and kindness, of humour, sympathy and an abiding Christian spirit.[80]

'It is given to few women', this writer added, 'to leave so unsullied a sense of sorrow.'

They had no children, and Carlo returned home alone, himself a sick man, to be cared for by his sister. He died less than a year later, and was buried in Westminster Abbey.

LADY WATERFORD

LOUISA STUART 'came out' in 1835, when she was seventeen, and her portrait was painted in that year by Hayter, who is said to have been dazzled by her beauty.[81] She had charm to add to her beauty, and her charm was enhanced by her talents and accomplishments; she drew and painted in watercolour with great proficiency, and she had a pleasant, rich contralto voice. All accounts agree, too, that she was becomingly modest.

In 1836 and 1837, she spent six months with her parents, Lord and Lady Stuart de Rothesay, in Italy, where she studied the great painters and - it seems - was particularly impressed by the Venetian masters of the sixteenth century. She broke the hearts of a succession of young men, and then, in 1839, she lost her own heart to a man with whom it was thought she could have nothing in common, Henry de la-Poer Beresford, 3rd Marquis of Waterford.

There was much in Lord Waterford's favour: he was young, and he had money and rank. On the other hand, he was a madcap, who had made a name for himself as a daredevil and a practical joker; and his greatest passion was for hunting. Lady Stuart de Rothesay found him boisterous, and deplored his lack of interest in anything that did not happen out of doors. Lou's sister, Char, tactfully agreed with her mother, but emphasized his qualities, specially his amiability and his generosity.

They had met and fallen in love at the medieval tournament staged by the Earl of Eglinton at his home, Eglinton Castle, Ayrshire. There was heavy rain on the day of the tournament, and the ground was turned into a quagmire. Few of the knights were prepared actually to enter the lists, but Lord Eglinton and Lord Waterford were among those few; and, jousting against each other, they brought some verisimilitude and excitement to the proceedings. In accordance with tradition, a Queen of Beauty was chosen, and there was a banquet and a ball. It was agreed that Lou was the most beautiful woman present, but - for some reason that is not now clear - it had been decided that the title must go to a married woman.[82]

They were married in 1842, by which time Lord Waterford had acquired a more sober image, and he took her to his home in the south of Ireland, Curraghmore, a grand house set in a vast estate - which Augustus Hare said was 'a territory rather than an estate'.[83] It was a happy marriage in every respect except in that, like the Cannings', it was childless. Waterford did not like to be away from Curraghmore, but in 1844 he took Lou to Carlsbad to 'take the waters', perhaps in the hope that it would help her to conceive; and he did not like Lou to be away from him, but he did not begrudge her own family the six weeks in the spring that she spent with them each year.

No sooner had Lou settled at Curraghmore than she was working, with Lord Waterford, to better the conditions of the tenants of the estate and the local people. It would be easy to caricature her as Lady Bountiful, but she was not proud or afraid of getting her hands dirty. And neither she nor Waterford was a dilettante. Both knew well that employment was better than charity, and they provided work for the men, chiefly as labourers, and for the women, some as domestics and others in a workshop for woollen goods, which was specially set up for them. A clothing club, started by Lou, became famous.

She was a deeply religious woman. She was a faithful member of the Church of England, and she transferred her loyalty to the Church of Ireland, though she was evidently disappointed to find that the Oxford Movement had not reached Curraghmore. Her churchmanship was later to change. She built two new churches nearby, and she, herself, designed and executed a set of stained-glass windows for one of them - not her first venture of this sort, since the original east window of the church at Highcliffe was her work. Leaving her marriage out of consideration, it would be true to say that nothing was more important to her than her religion and her art; and they were, in a sense, equally important: she regarded her art as a gift from God, held in trust.

In 1848, during one of her annual visits to England, her portrait was painted by Watts; and so began a life-long acquaintance between them, which she found instructive and both of them enjoyed. He was more and more impressed by her work as time went on.

> Of her genius for art he has said that he believed she
> was born an artist greater than any England has
> produced, the circumstances of her life alone preventing

her from working on to the full achievement. What work she did accomplish was, as far as it went, of the very highest order. Her brush full of colour, so unerringly blotting in all that she knew was essential to her subjects: these were always poetical, imaginative, and dignified, beautiful in colour and in arrangement of line. No faltering about truths of proportion and movement, or in the disposition of masses: nothing to jar as being out of keeping with the conception of her subjects.[84]

The portrait is perhaps the most appealing of the known likenesses of her.

It was probably a little later, in or about 1853, that she met Ruskin, with whose writings she was already familiar; and, through him, she met other writers and artists. She was to suggest that she did not like Ruskin personally,[85] but she valued his opinion as a critic, and they met and corresponded periodically for many years. He was not easy to please as a critic, indeed he could be brutal in his comments, but he always made it clear that he believed her capable of great work. It was important for her to make up her mind, he said, early in their acquaintance, whether she wished to be a grand lady amusing herself as an artist or an artist amusing herself as a grand lady.[86] And in the end he seems to have felt that she had made the wrong choice and failed herself; but he discounted the religious aspects of the matter, which were supremely important to her.

If the Venetians were not already models for Lou, they became such under Ruskin's tutelage. Having inspected some of her work, one day in 1857, he wrote to give her his opinion that it was good but not good enough.

> I seriously wonder how when you can do so much, you do not wish to get the full & tender quality of Titian as well as the power; Why, among these studies - is there no copy of Titian, or a bit of Titian - I should not care what model you took - Titian - or Veronese - or Tintoret or Giorgione - or Bassano - or Bellini - but I should like to see you setting yourself a higher standard by choosing one of them - and trying to do, here and there as well.[87]

Louisa, Marchioness of Waterford
by Sir Francis Grant
By courtesy of the National Portrait Gallery, London

In the following year, Lou went abroad with her mother; and in April and May they were in Venice.

Through Ruskin, she met the Pre-Raphaelites, Holman, Hunt, Millais and Rossetti, whose work she admired, though not uncritically. She and Char called on Hunt at his studio, one day in 1853, having been assured by Ruskin that they would be welcome, to see *The Light of the World*, which was standing there on an easel; and it may not have been surprising that they were oblivious to its setting, a room that had not been altered in any particular since the days of the artist's penury. 'It might have seemed that they had always lived with broken furniture by preference;' Hunt recorded, 'and when Lady Waterford, taking a chair by the back, placed her knee in the perforated seat, and so balanced her queenly person as she stood looking and talking, it might have been thought that the piece of furniture had been prepared for that especial purpose.'(88)

Hunt's considered opinion of Lou's work was delivered after her death. 'It came from the exercise of a very beautiful mind, and from a very diligently - although somewhat unmethodically - trained faculty for design,' he said, 'her taste for colour being also both remarkable by natural endowment, and by cultivation.' He regretted, however, that she was ' so humble in her regard for her designs that she did not take more pains to do them full justice - that is by drawing parts more correctly . ' (89)

Millais and Rossetti were both impressed. 'Yesterday morning, before going to the Derby,' Millais wrote to his wife in 1861, 'I called to see Lady Waterford and her drawings. She was so pleased, I think, for I found her drawings magnificent, so I could praise honestly.' He was blasé about the Derby, which he said was 'the usual crowd and dust'.(90) Rossetti admitted to Walter Severn, of the Dudley Gallery, that he had been dismayed when she had sent him a portfolio of her watercolours, with a request for his comments. Assuming that her work would not be in any way out of the ordinary he had simply ignored it for as long as possible. When, at last, he had opened the portfolio, he had been astonished. 'Need it be said that his repentance was sudden and complete', Severn remarked.(91)

Irish nationalism made itself felt like an earth tremor in 1843, the year of Lou's marriage, and again in 1848, when Curraghmore was shaken. In the years between, national aspirations, and all else except the daily struggle for survival, were driven from the minds of the Irish people by famine and starvation. They were years of stark tragedy.

The Act of Union between Ireland and England had come into force in 1801. Its purpose had been to complete Ireland's subjection to England, after centuries in which England had ruled only by right of conquest and Ireland had never submitted. In a vicious circle of action and reaction, which perpetuated bitter hostility, Ireland had resisted, sometimes alone and sometimes, when the opportunity had presented itself, by joining forces with England's enemies on the Continent of Europe, and had then faced grim retribution. The Union had been represented as an advantage to Ireland, particularly in commercial and economic terms, but it had proved disastrous, not least in those very terms.

In 1843, a campaign for the repeal of the Act of Union had come to its denouement. Its leader was Daniel O'Connell, a lawyer, and what he, himself, wanted for Ireland was self-government rather than independence, to be achieved by constitutional means; but not all his followers were of the same mind. The British Government was understandably nervous as mass-meetings took place in various parts of the country, largely well-ordered and peaceable but nevertheless ominous; and scattered acts of violence and destruction did occur. Lord Waterford was one of those who suffered, when the stables of his hunting lodge in Tipperary were burned down. Civil war was feared, and O'Connell was arrested and sent to prison. His conviction had been obtained on dubious grounds, and the House of Lords allowed an appeal against it, but by that time the campaign had lost its impetus.

In 1845, 1846 and again in 1848, blight destroyed the Irish potato crop, and with it the Irish people's means of subsistence. Government, that is the government at Westminster, was committed to a *laissez-faire* policy, though the presuppositions on which that policy was based, whether or not they were valid for England, were not valid for Ireland, and the relief that was provided was woefully inadequate. Even when ministers woke to the fact that men, women and children, whom the Act of Union had made their fellow-countrymen, were starving to death, they granted no more additional aid than they reckoned was necessary to save themselves from scandal, taking the view that Ireland should solve its problems out of its own resources.

The notion that Ireland could solve its problems out of its own resources was embodied in the Labour Rate Act. This made landlords financially responsible for their destitute tenants, a piece of legislation that was at best unrealistic and at worst self-defeating. As Cecil Woodham-Smith has said, 'few classes of men have had so much abuse heaped on them as Irish landlords, and with justification',(92) but some were themselves ruined by the failures of the potato crop, since their income came from rents and rents could not be paid. Many landlords, however, evaded their responsibilities by one means or another, most cruelly by turning their tenants out of their homes and off the land.

There was nothing new about evictions: it was simply that they became more common during the famine. Early in 1846, before the Labour Rate Act came into force, Daniel O'Connell's son, John, an M.P., attacked Lord Waterford in the House of Commons for supposedly having driven out the population of an entire village. It was shown that O'Connell's information was incorrect, and that both Lord Waterford and Lou deserved praise rather than criticism. O'Connell later expressed his regrets to the House, but he did not stop at that. 'I wish to add one word on this subject,' he said.

> I am anxious to bear my willing testimony to the merits of the Marquess of Waterford as a resident landlord. It would not be in my power to use language sufficiently strong to express my sense of the merits of that most estimable lady (the Marchioness of Waterford), who has been alluded to. ... Her charities are most considerate, well managed and abundant; and the Marquess of Waterford is certainly one of the best landlords in Ireland.(93)

Homelessness and starvation were not the only horrors to which the people were exposed. Epidemics of the diseases associated with malnutrition and unhygienic conditions swept the country, and the winter of 1846-1847 was the most severe in living memory. In some areas, the authorities were reduced to such a state of helplessness that civilisation virtually broke down. Emigration was the only escape for hundreds of thousands of people, who took their hostility towards England with them wherever they went.

There were sporadic outbreaks of violence throughout these years, and revenge killings of landlords, particularly in 1847, conjured up the spectre of a mass rising of the starving masses. But when a rising took place in 1848, it was led by men of the class to which Daniel O'Connell had belonged. These men, who called their movement 'Young Ireland', were inspired by the revolutionary events that were taking place on the Continent of Europe, but they, themselves, were not made of revolutionary material; they were intellectuals and romantics, rather than men of action or realists, and their campaign, though full of sound and fury, achieved nothing and ended almost in farce.

Futile as 'Young Ireland' proved to be, Lou and Lord Waterford found themselves in danger from the movement at Curraghmore in 1848, and Lou spent part of that year in England with her mother, at his insistence. The situation had not improved when she persuaded him to allow her to come back, and Curraghmore was fortified and garrisoned. Reliable information about the threats that they faced was difficult to come by, but rumours abounded. It was said that he or she, or both of them, were to be kidnapped and held hostage for the safety of the leaders of the movement, and that the house was to be burned down. A nearby police station was attacked, with some loss of life, and Waterford was warned to expect an attack on Curraghmore at any moment, but time passed without any further trouble; and, eventually, it became clear that the emergency was over.

Lou did not waste her time while she was shut up in the fortress that Curraghmore had become. She had produced illustrations for a new edition of *The Babes in the Wood*, and she occupied herself in preparing her work for publication. The book was published in London in 1849.

The effects of the famine were cumulative, so that its full force was still being felt in 1849, when Queen Victoria visited Ireland with Prince Albert. Strong arguments had been advanced both in favour of the visit and against it; but, in terms of the welcome that the Queen received and the pleasure that she gave, it was an undoubted success. Its social high point was a 'drawing-room' at Dublin Castle, and Lou and Lord Waterford were there, among an immense throng of notables. They were present, too, at a *déjeuner*, given for the Queen by the Duke of Leinster at his home, Carton, outside Dublin, and Lou found herself, during part of the proceedings, sitting between the Lord-Lieutenant, the Earl of Clarendon, and Prince Albert.

Arrivals at Dublin Castle for the 'drawing-room' were obliged to wait their turn in a queue of carriages, exposed to the quizzing of a crowd of onlookers. It was a good-natured crowd, however, and the police had caught its mood. 'We had tremendous cheers for "the markis", and another cheer for the "marchioness",' Lou reported to her mother. 'The policemen amused us, keeping off the people and saying, "You may have one look, and then move on".'(94)

There followed several years of comparative calm and contentment for the Waterfords; and then, in 1859, Lord Waterford was killed in a hunting accident. Lou had always been afraid of such an accident, but that did not make the blow any more bearable when it came. Her religion, however, was a great comfort to her.

She had lost her home with the loss of her husband, since all Lord Waterford's Irish property passed to his brother with the title; but Ford Castle, in Northumberland, came to her, for her lifetime. She knew Ford, having stayed there frequently with Waterford, and she was already fond of it.

Lady Stuart de Rothesay had been widowed in 1845, and mother and daughter were now frequently together again, at Ford or Highcliffe or in London. They went abroad together in 1860, travelling in France, Italy and Germany. At Ford, Lou began at once to show the interest in the tenants of the estate and the local people that she had shown at Curraghmore, with the difference that here she was in charge; and she soon set out on an ambitious programme of improvements to the Castle - a medieval building, heavily Gothicized after the fashion of Strawberry Hill - and the estate. The village school that she built then was to be decorated by her, over a period of more than twenty years, with some of her best work - murals, which she called frescoes - and to become, later, for that reason, a fitting memorial to her.

Char's death came in 1861, and it drew Lou and her mother even more closely together, so that when Lady Stuart de Rothesay, herself, died in 1867 Lou felt completely bereft. From that time onwards, increasingly, she referred in her letters to her loneliness; few women in her position can have had so many devoted friends, but what she missed was the constant, close companionship to which she had been accustomed.

Highcliffe came to her when Lady Stuart de Rothesay died, and for the rest of her own life she divided each year between her two homes, usually spending the summer at Highcliffe and the winter at Ford. It seemed to her that Highcliffe and Ford, like her art, had been entrusted to her by God, and that she had a special responsibility, under God, for those who were dependent on her in any way in Hampshire or Northumberland. Her art continued to engross her attention, but only to the extent to which the working out of her Christian faith allowed, or to which it might be made to serve the Church. 'I could not live for art,' she once said. 'It would not be what I was put into the world to do. Two homes have been given to me, and it is that I may try to do what I can in them, that they are mine for "brief life".'(95)

By this time, there had been a change in Lou's orientation within the Church of England. As a young woman, she had seen the Church as a Divine institution, with bishops who derived their authority directly from the Apostles and formularies which were to be regarded as sacrosanct. It was the Church of the Oxford Movement. Now, for her, the Bible was the main source of authority, and the preaching of the Gospel was more important than the observance of rites and ceremonies. She had descended from the High Church to the Low Church.

The series of murals in the village school at Ford, which illustrates stories of children from the Bible, ranks as her greatest artistic achievement, at least in terms of its concept and scope. If she ever explained exactly why she painted these pictures, there is no record of what she had to say. Perhaps she simply wanted succeeding generations of pupils to be surrounded by images of innocence and virtue, as some writers have suggested; but Michael Joicey, one of Lou's successors at Ford, who made a study of her work, thought otherwise. For Lord Joicey, there was a recurring theme in the murals: 'that faith in a loving and all-powerful God triumphs in the end over (the) evil ways of men, but that this faith must be taught and worked for both by children and parents ...'(96)

The murals were not accessible to a wide public, and Lou would not have considered that they should be. Little of her work was ever shown in public, and that was in accordance with the conventions of her day and class. Ladies, who used watercolours rather than oils, mounted their work in albums or collected it in folios, which were shown to their families and friends, and only occasionally sent it to exhibitions. In any case, the art establishment, as embodied, in particular, by the Royal Academy, did little to encourage women artists or watercolourists.

The Royal Academy, indeed, was an exclusive and hidebound institution, which did little to forward the cause of art in any way, and it was not only those who had reputations to make who thought so then; Watts and Whistler were among the critics. But times were changing, and one of the facilitators of change was Lou's second-cousin Sir Coutts Lindsay, Bart., who opened the Grosvenor Gallery in Bond Street in 1877. Here was exhibited whatever Lindsay considered worthwhile or interesting, in any medium by any artist; chiefly, but not exclusively, contemporary work. The setting was magnificent, and Lindsay's connections, social and artistic, gave the exhibitions great prestige. 'The Grosvenor Gallery was the most celebrated private gallery to be set up for the display of paintings and works of art in England in the second half of the nineteenth century.'[97]

There were examples of Lou's work in the summer exhibition at the Grosvenor Gallery every year from 1878 to 1882: four in 1878; three in 1879; three in 1880; three in 1881; and two in 1882. They were usually hung in the Watercolour Gallery, but two, one in 1879 and the other in 1881, were shown in the West Gallery, the main exhibition space.[98] She was always self-deprecatory about what she did; she never thought her work compared well with that of other women at the Grosvenor Gallery exhibitions, but the critics do not appear to have taken the same view of it. Relatively few women, as it happened, saw themselves represented in the West Gallery.

She also exhibited at the Dudley Gallery in Piccadilly, which was founded in 1865 for watercolourists; and a clerical error made there in the use of her name produced an interesting result. Her name appeared in the 1887 exhibition catalogue as Mr. L. Waterford, and a critic, who should have known of her existence, by this time, if no more about her, failed to notice the mistake. He praised the picture that she was exhibiting in fulsome terms for its Titianesque quality, and then asked, 'Who is Mr. Waterford, this new genius, reviving the glories of the Venetian School?'[99] The story is given added piquancy by the fact that this critic had censured the gallery for showing the work of amateurs.

Lou liked to visit the London exhibitions, but she did not like London. Her preference for the country did not prejudice her social life, however, as her letters and the Highcliffe Visitors' Book testify.* A list of

---

*   Visitors' Book. National Art Library, Victoria & Albert Museum, London. 42.QQ.134

her friends would be a long one, but among the closest were Lady Jane Bouverie, later Lady Jane Ellice, Lady Marian Alford and Miss Honoria Thompson. The Countess of Tankerville, her neighbour at Ford, must be mentioned, if only because they collaborated in the illustration of a book called *Life Songs*, which was published in 1884.[100] Gladstone must be mentioned, too, since they knew each other well, and she was evidently a Liberal in her politics.[101]

The Prince and Princess of Wales made the trip from Osborne to Highcliffe, with their children, in the royal yacht, in 1880, 1881 and again in 1885, accompanied in 1881 by Crown Princess Victoria of Germany and Prussia, the Prince's sister, and her children. King Oscar II and Queen Sophia of Sweden and Norway stayed at Highcliffe in 1881, following a visit by Crown Prince Gustaf, with Augustus Hare, in 1879. Lou visited Queen Sophia of the Netherlands in 1870, and the Queen came to Ford in 1872.

In the summer of 1890, Lou was invited to Osborne. She was then seventy-two and Queen Victoria seventy-one.' I have actually been on a visit to Osborne - to dine and sleep.' she wrote to a friend. 'I specially enjoyed it: indeed I did much want to see the Queen again, and was agreeably surprised to see her looking so well, such a smooth face, and, if wider in figure, not strikingly so: her expression is really charming with the old attraction of "le regard caressant".[102] She had been asked to take a portfolio of her drawings with her, and she found it displayed in the drawing-room. The Queen expressed particular admiration for a picture called *Relentless Time*, which, of course, Lou begged her to accept.

The visit to Osborne was the last visit that she ever made. She was unwell when she moved from Highcliffe to Ford later that year, and it was at Ford, in 1891, that she died. Her last words to one of her friends are said to have been: 'Beauty and goodness, goodness and beauty, those are ever the great things!'[103] The sentiment seems cloying a century later, but it was genuine; beauty and goodness were always the qualities by which she set most store. Her cousin, General Charles Stuart, quoted the fourth chapter of St. Paul's letter to the Philippians as her rule of life.[104]

> Finally, brethren, whatsoever things are true, what-
> soever things are honest, whatsoever things are pure,
> whatsoever things are lovely, whatsoever things are of

good report: if there be any virtue, and if there be any praise, think on these things.

A year after her death, an exhibition of her work was held at Carlton House Terrace, just along the row from the house in which she had lived before her marriage. The drawing-room of this house was full of pictures and sketches representative of her *oeuvre*, that is watercolours, with or without body colour, and chiefly figures. Watts visited the exhibition. 'He went many times,' his wife recorded, 'and at each visit his admiration increased. "She never makes a mistake in movement, in proportion, or in expression," was his answer to those who cavilled at what they considered a want of correct drawing.'[105] Henry James, who was moved to ecstasies of reverential circumlocution by his memories of her at a dinner-party, wrote more or less plainly of the wonderful colour that blazed down from the walls of the room.

Lou's murals can still be seen at what was the village school at Ford, and is now the Lady Waterford Hall. The Victoria and Albert Museum and the Tate Gallery both possess examples of her watercolours, as does the National Trust at Belton House; the Royal Collection, at Windsor, contains others.

GENERAL CHARLES STUART
Charles Stuart III

CHARLES STUART III, the son of Captain John Stuart, R.N., was a soldier, and he lived to attain the rank of a full general, outranking both his father and his grandfather, Lieutenant-General Sir Charles Stuart, Charles Stuart I. Ironically, however, though he was on active service when he was first commissioned, it is unlikely that he ever saw action or even heard a shot fired in anger. Much of the available information about his military career comes from Army Lists and regimental archives; it is incomplete, and in the case of the Army Lists it is not entirely reliable.

Information about his life otherwise is not plentiful, and it varies widely in biographical value. Standard reference books show that he was born in 1810, and that his father died almost exactly a year later. His father's will tells us that his uncle, Charles Stuart II, later Lord Stuart de Rothesay, and his maternal grandfather, John Sullivan, were made trustees of the property that was to be his when he came of age; and it seems reasonable to infer from the facts that there was a warm relationship between him and his uncle, who may have seen in him the son that he never had.

Reference books also show that he went to Harrow, and the school archives reveal that he was sent there in 1820 but removed three years later. Two surviving letters from his mother to his uncle, written in the autumn of 1823, tell us more: Mrs. Stuart wrote from Hubborne House, on the northern edge of the Highcliffe estate, later known as Hoburne Lodge (his home for many years), and it can be deduced from what she said that the house had been part of his father's property. She wrote of moving to a farmhouse at Westover, a place that was to be swallowed up by Bournemouth, for the sake of economy; and she wrote, too, of a new school for him, perhaps, like the farmhouse, a matter of economy.[106]

Mrs. Stuart married again in 1825. Her second husband was a clergyman, the Reverend Marmaduke Thompson. Sadly, however, she died two years later.

Charles obtained a commission in the 4th (King's Own) Regiment of Foot at the age of sixteen, late in the year 1826, when Britain was caught up in a crisis in the affairs of Portugal. It was a crisis about the background to which, as it happened, nobody knew more than his uncle. The young queen, Maria, faced an attempt by her uncle, Miguel, to seize the throne, and the Regent, her aunt, Isabella, called on Britain to come to her aid, invoking long-standing treaties. At first, Britain declined to act, on the ground that the treaties in question dealt with foreign aggression and not internal dissension or civil war. Then Miguel launched attacks on Portugal from Spain, with Spanish backing, and Britain could not stand back any longer.

George Canning was Foreign Secretary, and this was one of the great moments of his career. Addressing the House of Commons, he declared that to keep faith with the nation's allies and to safeguard the nation's honour was more important than to avoid the risk of war; and then he announced that British troops were already on their way to the ports of embarkation for Portugal. 'We go to plant the standard of England on the well-known heights of Lisbon,' he declaimed, at the end of his speech. 'Where that standard is planted, foreign dominion shall not come.'[107]

The King's Own was sent to Portugal as part of the British force, with Charles as one of its most junior officers. But, though he had only just obtained his commission, he had the advantage of being known to the commander of the force, General Sir William Clinton. Charles' grandfather had fought with Sir William's father in the American War, and his grandmother had not scrupled to have the General's attention drawn to the fact. Whatever, exactly, was the result of this manoeuvre, it pleased Charles' family, not least, apparently, because it was done on the basis that he would be helped if he would help himself.[108]

In Portugal, in 1827 and the early part of 1828, he rubbed shoulders with veterans of the American and French wars and Waterloo, and perhaps he envied them their experiences; but if he dreamed of action he was disappointed: the presence of the British force, and a cautionary word from France to Spain, persuaded Miguel and his friends to change their tactics. What they could not achieve by force they eventually achieved by intrigue, but not before they had plunged Portugal into civil war again; and by that time Britain had a new Prime Minister, Wellington, who - having seen and heard enough of the Peninsula - was glad to be able to bring the troops home.

Charles had had to purchase his commission*, and he had to purchase each step up to the rank of lieutenant-colonel. He obtained a lieutenancy in the King's Own in 1828, and then, in 1829, he transferred to the 1st (Grenadier) Regiment of Foot, a move in which the influence of the Clintons can be detected, since Sir William's son, Frederick, was a Grenadier, and they had become friends in Portugal. James II gave the Guards the privilege of a double rank system in 1687, allowing them the pay of the higher rank for the duties of the lower one, and Charles transferred as Ensign and Lieutenant. In 1832, he was made Lieutenant and Captain, but this was the year of the Reform Bill, and his military career was interrupted by a brief excursion into politics.

Parliamentary reform was a matter that greatly concerned Charles' family, and it was the subject of much discussion between his uncle, by this time raised to the peerage as Lord Stuart de Rothesay, and the 2nd Marquess of Bute, head of the Stuart family.[109] Lord Bute was afraid that it foreshadowed the end of the monarchy. In the first elections held under the provisions of the Reform Acts for England and Scotland, however, the constituency of Buteshire was found to be safe in the Stuarts' pocket. Charles was persuaded to stand - in the Conservative interest, it may be needless to say - and he was returned unopposed.[110]

The First Reformed Parliament, which met at the beginning of 1833, did not differ in composition from earlier parliaments as much as had been expected, and the new radical and maverick members caused surprisingly little excitement, once the novelty of their presence had worn off. In retrospect at least, therefore, this parliament was memorable for the sense of anticlimax that attached to it; but it deserves to be remembered for two important Acts, one abolishing slavery and the other limiting the hours of work for children in factories. Whatever Charles thought of all this, he seems soon to have decided that Parliament was not for him, since he applied for the Chiltern Hundreds that same summer.

*A note in the Highcliffe Parish Magazine for July 1892 has it that this was a non-purchase commission, granted by the Duke of York as Commander-in-Chief.

A reasonable supposition is that the army drew him back, and it is a fact that he became Adjutant of the 1st Battalion of the Grenadiers at just this time. But he was becoming increasingly drawn to travel, and - whether as cause or effect - it was becoming increasingly clear, at the same time, that he was not destined for a glittering military career. Perhaps he was not ambitious; and perhaps, for him, the army was less a profession than a gentlemanly occupation. Be that as it may, in 1834 he spent two months in Switzerland and that part of the Emperor of Austria's dominions that included Venice,[111] and in the following year he set out on an extended visit to Persia and Turkey, an account of which was later published.[112]

The occasion for the visit was the accession of a new shah to the Peacock Throne of Persia, and the dispatch of a special diplomatic mission to mark it. The head of the mission, Henry Ellis, was related to the Stuarts, and it was arranged that he should take Charles with him as his private secretary. Ellis's departure was delayed, and Charles set out ahead of him in order to make the most of the journey. He chose to return to Venice and to continue the journey by sea, but he was obliged to make use of whatever craft happened to be available at the ports at which he called, so that the voyage was, at times, both uncomfortable and dangerous. He spent some time in the Ionian Islands, of which he was soon to see more under other circumstances, and saw the sights of Athens; and he kept a pre-arranged rendezvous with Ellis at Constantinople.

Ellis's mission was to Persia, but he travelled as an ambassador and was received as such at Constantinople, so that his party, which now included Charles, found doors open to them that were not open to ordinary visitors; and Charles did not fail to take advantage of the change in his status to see as much of the place and its people as possible. Favoured as they were in this respect, however, there and elsewhere in their travels, their onward journey through Turkey and Persia, on hired hacks, often with no proper shelter at night, was no more comfortable or free from danger than had been Charles' voyage from Venice.

They were accorded full honours at Tehran, their journey's end. Charles was present at Ellis's audience with the Shah, at which His Excellency offered His Majesty, on behalf of the King of England, condolences on the death of his predecessor - which may have been superfluous - and congratulations on his own accession; and then, while

Ellis held discussions with the Shah and his ministers on various matters of importance to Britain and Persia, he and others of the party together explored the city and neighbouring parts of the country. His duties as Ellis's private secretary do not appear to have detained him for long.

He travelled back to England with Ellis, when the mission was over. They planned to mitigate the rigours of travel in Persia and Turkey by taking a paddle-steamer from Trebizond to Constantinople, but they made an unfortunate choice. According to Charles, who was not given to extravagant travellers' tales, the steamer had lost the use of a paddle and the captain had lost the use of an arm and a leg. And the captain is supposed to have said to Charles: 'Ah, I have not felt well since I helped that poor fellow on deck who died of the plague last month!'[113] From Constantinople to Odessa, they entrusted themselves to another steamer; and from Odessa, they crossed Europe in a rickety carriage, via Warsaw and Berlin, to Hamburg. Charles finally reached London late in 1836, after eighteen months away from his regiment.

Sometime in 1837, he was off again, this time as Extra A.D.C. to the High Commissioner for the Ionian Islands, General Sir Howard Douglas. These seven islands, of which Corfu is probably the best known, lie in what was for centuries a strategically important position, off the coast of Greece, between Greece and Italy, and they changed hands repeatedly as a consequence. They were annexed by Napoleon in 1807, placed under British protection in 1815, by the Treaty of Paris, and ceded to Greece in 1864. Sir Howard's period of office was notable for his attempts to better the lot of the islanders, and for the hostility that he met with from them. Charles was in the islands for a year, but it is a year for which, otherwise, we have no account of him at all.

There is a letter from Charles to his uncle, written in the summer of 1835, when he was on his way to meet Ellis at Constantinople, in which he mentioned a certain Miss Gore. 'I was in hopes,' he wrote, 'that travelling would have cured my love for Miss Gore, but the result has been rather the contrary!'[114] She was Georgiana, usually known as Minny, daughter of Vice-Admiral Sir John Gore, and she was entitled to be addressed as the Honourable Miss Gore because she had been a maid of honour to Queen Adelaide. Four years later, in 1839, Charles and Minny were married. They were to have one child, a son, John, who died in infancy.

General Charles Stuart
As Captain Charles Stuart, M.P.
Detail from 'The House of Commons, 1833'
by Sir George Hayter
By courtesy of the National Portrait Gallery, London

There follow years for which we have only fragmentary accounts of him. In 1843, he travelled to St. Petersburg to visit Lord Stuart de Rothesay, British Ambassador since 1841, who was ill; and he offered to return to Russia to escort his uncle home, when he resigned in 1844, but it was evidently unnecessary for him to do so. He was Brigade Major, Northern District, at the end of 1844 and the beginning of 1845, and at the beginning of 1845 he was made Captain and Lieutenant-Colonel. But then, in 1846, he transferred from the Grenadiers to the 13th (Prince Albert's Somersetshire) Light Infantry.

Charles' transfer gave him the command of the 13th Light Infantry. He became a general in due course, but he was never given a more important command. The history of the regiment tells us that he was a capable and effective commanding officer, and that he combined firm discipline with an unusual degree of concern for his men. In some respects, indeed, according to the author of the history, he was ahead of his time, particularly in the establishment of regimental libraries and schools; and we are told, too, that Mrs. Stuart - Minny - took a personal interest in the schools.[115]

The 13th were based in Ireland from 1847 to 1850, though references to the famine and 'Young Ireland' are conspicuous by their absence from the history of the regiment; and Charles and Minny paid several visits to the Waterfords at Curraghmore during this period. From 1850 to 1851 they were based in Scotland, and in 1851 they were sent to Gibraltar, where they still were in 1853, at the outbreak of the Crimean War. Britain and France, seeing that their interests lay in supporting Turkey against Russia, entered the war in 1854, and the 13th were sent to the Crimea in 1855. But Charles had to resign his command, on grounds of ill-health, at the end of 1854.

Earlier in that year, 1854, he had been promoted to the rank of colonel, and he saw out the war, once his health had sufficiently improved, as one of the colonels on the staff of the new military establishment at Aldershot, where a training camp had been set up. It must have been in or about 1855 that he settled at Hoburne Lodge, with Minny, since he was said to have lived in the parish for thirty-seven years at the time of his death in 1892,[116] and he is referred to as 'Colonel Stuart of Hubborne Lodge' in a document of 1856, concerning his purchase of adjoining land.[117] Highcliffe, the house that his uncle had built, was no more than a mile away, across a common.

74

But Charles settled at Hoburne only in the sense that he made it his home. During the Indian Mutiny, he was appointed Military Secretary to the Governor-General of India, Lord Canning, and he arrived at Calcutta, with Minny, a few days before Christmas 1857. He was welcomed not only as a member of Lord Canning's staff but also as Lady Canning's cousin; and Minny was welcomed, too, as a friend with whom Lady Canning could throw off the restraints of protocol. Lady Canning had need of such a friend, though she had no use for a confidante.

Charles served Canning throughout the remainder of the emergency, and was with him at Allahabad for the greater part of the year 1858, while Minny was with Lady Canning in the Nilgiri Hills. Canning had exchanged Calcutta for Allahabad in order to be as closely in touch as possible with the military operations in that part of India, particularly at Lucknow, capital of the State of Oudh. Before these operations were completed, he drew up plans for dealing with the mutineers and rebels who would face his justice; and he published his intentions in the Proclamation of Oudh, which provoked a furore in India and in England.

Canning attracted much criticism for his policies in India, most of it ill-founded, but no other single item of policy caused such controversy as one of those contained in the Proclamation of Oudh; this was to make forfeit the property of the treacherous landowners of the State. Nothing, the argument ran, could have been better calculated to stiffen the resistance of these men and others who depended on them. The counter-argument rested on context and interpretation; and, as far as interpretation at least was concerned, Charles was in a position to keep the record straight. He had been charged with the responsibility of informing the appropriate officials that the Governor-General favoured liberality.[118]

Charles took part in the ceremonies and, with Minny, joined in the celebrations at Allahabad at the end of 1858, when the Queen assumed the Government of India as Empress and Canning became Viceroy. And at Calcutta again in 1859 he and Minny were able to celebrate, with the Cannings, the return of peace to India. Peace and the viceroyalty added several degrees of grandeur to the Cannings' lives, and Charles described some of the great occasions at which he was present. On the Queen's birthday in 1859 there was a military parade, a levée and a ball.

75

The ball at night was in high-state. We met the Viceroy and Charlotte in the council room, whence they came upstairs in procession, the household servants, officers of the body-guard, and personal staff preceding them. A guard of honour of the 99th, with a colour, was drawn up at the north end of the ball-room, facing the throne. In the ball-room, we opened into two lines, facing inwards, and the 'august pair', looking extremely grand and high-bred, walked through us to the canopy.[119]

Lady Canning was invariably kind and appreciative in what she had to say about Charles and Minny in letters, but not so Johny Stanley, one of Canning's A.D.C.s, at least not as far as Minny was concerned. Stanley was a flippant young man, but his shafts may not always have been wide of the mark; and, as he pointed out in one of his letters to his mother, Lady Canning never spoke ill of anyone. He found Minny manipulative and meddlesome, and he laughed at what he saw as her self-importance. 'What do I care if she was a maid of honour. It proves nothing. Besides, no one could help knowing it. She keeps Hon'ble before her name even now, and was absurd enough to have it stuck on all her tin boxes.'[120] Religiosity seems to have been one of her tiresome characteristics.

By the end of the summer of 1859, the Stuarts had returned to England; and soon afterwards there began the series of events that was to lead to Charles' involvement in a *cause célèbre* in English and Scottish law. The 2nd Marquess of Bute, Charles' second cousin, had died in 1848, when his son John Patrick, who had become 3rd Marquess, was only six months old, and the Court of Chancery in England had made his wife the child's guardian. But in 1859 the Marchioness died, leaving in her will the recommendation that Charles and a certain Lady Elizabeth Moore should be appointed joint guardians in her place. The Court of Chancery approved this recommendation; and it was agreed between the new guardians that John Patrick should be cared for by Charles and Minny, and should be sent to an English school.

When Charles went to Mount Stuart, the Scottish home of the Marquesses of Bute, to take charge of John Patrick, Lady Elizabeth begged him not to take the boy away and promised to bring him to London herself. She did bring him to London, but evidently in the hope of furthering a scheme which would have allowed her to have charge of him, after all; and when Charles, having got wind of this scheme, asked for the Court of Chancery's authority to proceed with his own plans, based on the original agreement, she spirited him back to Scotland and out of English judicial jurisdiction. She refused to give him up when Charles followed them back to Scotland with the Court of Chancery's authority in due form, and refused again when the Court deprived her of her guardianship and positively ordered her to hand him over.

The Court of Session in Edinburgh was then asked to intervene on Charles' behalf, but it declined to do so, on several grounds, one of which was that no precise precedent could be found. The fact of the matter was, however, that the Scottish court did not wish to see a Scot handed over to a guardian appointed by an English court. Finally, an appeal was made to the House of Lords, the highest court in England and Scotland, and its judgement was delivered by the Lord Chancellor, Lord Brougham - a Scottish lawyer. Having reviewed the case, Brougham concluded that the Court of Session was wrong, so that its decision must be reversed and the question of an appeal did not arise.[121] The judgement confirmed Charles as John Patrick's sole guardian.

More was to be heard of the 3rd Marquess of Bute, if only because his rank and wealth gave his actions an interest that would not otherwise have attached to them. He became a Catholic as a young man just down from Oxford, and the significance of that step at that time is difficult to understand now. Gerard Manley Hopkins was converted at about the same time, and one of his biographers has written: 'In 1866 a man was shaken loose from his position in society if he became a Catholic'.[122] For the rest of his life he was totally preoccupied with his religion in all its aspects, including the most arcane. Others were fascinated by the story, and it provided Disraeli with the basis for his novel *Lothair*.

Charles was promoted to the rank of major-general in 1860, while the guardianship case was going through the courts; the case was not over until the middle of the next year. In 1862, he was appointed Vice-Lieutenant for Buteshire. The Scottish lieutenancy, like its English equivalent, was originally set up to raise the militia at times of national emergency, and by Charles' day it was a permanent organisation consisting of a lord-lieutenant, a vice-lieutenant and a varying number of deputy-lieutenants in each county, though its functions were gradually becoming more ceremonial than practical. Charles was Vice-Lieutenant for the rest of his life.

His military career was over, to all intents and purposes, by this time. While he held the rank of colonel his name appeared in the lists of colonels with the note that he was attached to the Ceylon Rifle Regiment, and this is difficult to explain, since his name did not appear in the lists of officers of the regiment. The regiment served chiefly in Ceylon, and he is not known to have been to the island. In 1868 he was promoted to the rank of lieutenant-general, and in 1870 he was made honorary Colonel of the 46th (South Devonshire) Regiment of Foot. The 46th was amalgamated with the 32nd (Cornwall) Light Infantry in 1881, to form the 1st and 2nd Battalions of the Duke of Cornwall's Light Infantry, and he became Colonel of the 2nd Battalion.

It was seniority that brought him promotion now, and in 1875, a few weeks after his sixty-fifth birthday, he was made a general. His duties as Vice-Lieutenant of Buteshire and Colonel of the 46th took him away from home occasionally, and he continued to travel, 'his favourite sojournings', we are told, 'being (in) Italy, Switzerland, Egypt and the Holy Land',[123] but Hoburne and Highcliffe - the place - were claiming more of his time and interest. By 1875, Highcliffe - the house - had passed to his cousin Louisa, Lady Waterford, though she spent only the summers there; she spent the winters at Ford Castle.

It was said that Charles was more like a brother than a cousin to Lady Waterford in her widowhood,[124] and Lady Waterford made a close friend of Minny, visiting her almost daily in the last years of her life, when she was an invalid, always walking across the common between Highcliffe and Hoburne. Minny died in 1877, and in 1878 Charles married Louisa Murdoch. Charles and Lady Waterford shared a religious faith, one of the expressions of which was a concern for the communities in which they lived, and Charles took a particular interest in the church and the schools. He was a generous benefactor to Highcliffe parish church; and he bore a large part of the cost of building the first local schools, in the management of which he was involved for many years afterwards.[125]

He died at Hoburne in 1892, the year following the death of Lady Waterford, and was buried in the churchyard at Highcliffe. His vision had been failing for sometime, a great sadness to him, since he enjoyed books and had a large library, but we are told that he maintained his 'upright and soldier-like bearing' to the last.[(126)]

GENERAL EDWARD STUART WORTLEY

WE ARE TOLD that Edward Stuart Wortley had met Lady Waterford only twice before, on both occasions years earlier, when he paid her a visit in 1889 and was told that he was to inherit Highcliffe.[127] Though they cannot have known each other well, they were related through John Stuart, 3rd Earl of Bute.

Lord Bute's second son, James Archibald, was Edward's great-great grandfather, and his fourth son, Charles, was Lady Waterford's grandfather. James Archibald's son, another James Archibald, was raised to the peerage as 1st Baron Wharncliffe, and this James Archibald's grandson, Edward, the 3rd Baron, was given two steps in the peerage to become 1st Earl of Wharncliffe. The 1st Earl's heir was his brother, Francis, who predeceased him, and it was Francis's son, also Francis, who became the 2nd Earl. Meanwhile, the family name had been varied several times. Edward Stuart Wortley, whose simple variant of the name was used by him without a hyphen, was the 2nd Earl's younger brother.

Most of the information that we have about him comes from three sources: standard reference books, for his family background; Army Lists, for the essential facts of his career; and his wife's books of autobiography and reminiscence for the rest.[128&129] He was born in 1857. His father was the Honourable Francis Montagu-Stuart-Wortley, and his mother was Maria, daughter of William Martin, of Worsborough Hall in Yorkshire. He went to Eton when he was seven, and his military career began when, at eighteen, he joined an Irish militia regiment, the Kildare Rifles. At twenty, however, he transferred to the King's Royal Rifle Corps, and was sent to India.

He was soon in action, in the Afghan War of 1878-1880. Russian influence in Afghanistan and north-west India had caused Britain anxiety for many years, and when, in 1878, a Russian mission was received by the Amir at Kabul and a British mission was not, a full-scale invasion was launched. The Amir died and was succeeded by his son, who was obliged to give Britain control of his country's defence and foreign policy, with a British minister at Kabul. Then Afghan soldiers, said to be mutinous, massacred the minister and his entire mission, and fighting began again. This time, after a campaign best remembered for General Sir Frederick Roberts' celebrated march from Kabul to Kandahar, the new Amir abdicated, and the country was occupied until it could safely be handed over to another member of the ruling family.

From India, in 1881, Eddy's battalion was sent to South Africa, to join the British force that was facing a Boer uprising in the Transvaal. Britain had annexed this Boer state in 1877, and the uprising had taken place in 1880. But the confrontation had come to an end with the ignominious and bloody defeat of the British at Majuba Hill, before the reinforcements could reach them; and, in a scrap of reminiscence, from which his wife quotes in her books, Eddy has less to say about the reason for his presence in South Africa than about an incident in which he unwittingly let pass a chance of becoming exceedingly rich. He and a friend were offered a large tract of land for a song and turned it down, only to find, later, that it was part of what was, by then, the Witwatersrand gold-field.

An association with Egypt and the Sudan began for him in the Anglo-Egyptian War of 1882. Egypt had been brought to the brink of bankruptcy by debts to British and French banks, and Britain had been alarmed, not only by the risk to the banks of substantial losses, but also by the possibility of risk to the security of the Suez Canal. Such was Egypt's plight that the Khedive agreed to allow British and French officials to take over the management of the country's financial affairs; but what was seen as foreign interference, in these and other matters, was much resented, and the army staged what amounted to a coup. All British and French interests were now under threat, and their nationals in the country demanded protection.

Britain had to act alone: Egypt was part of the Ottoman Empire - and the Khedive was the Sultan's Viceroy, but Turkey no longer had the power to intervene effectively; and France was fully committed elsewhere in North Africa. The first move was made by the Royal Navy, which interpreted the activities of the Egyptian Army on the coast as hostile and bombarded and occupied Alexandria. Then a British Expeditionary Force, under the command of General Sir Garnet Wolseley, landed at Ismailia, on the Suez Canal, and won a decisive victory at Tel-el-Kebir. Eddy acted as Orderly Officer to General Sir Baker Russell, who commanded the cavalry, at Tel-el-Kebir, and he joined in the cavalry's pursuit of the enemy to Cairo after the battle.

Responsibility for the government of Egypt now rested fairly and squarely with Britain, and with it responsibility for Egypt's vassal state, the Sudan. Sir Evelyn Baring, later Lord Cromer, was made governor, though out of deference to the Sultan and the Khedive he was given the title of Resident, and General Sir Evelyn Wood, V.C., was appointed Commander-in-Chief or Sirdar of the new Egyptian Army. Eddy became A.D.C. to Sir Evelyn Wood, and in that capacity, early in 1884, he met General Charles Gordon, who stayed with the Sirdar in Cairo on his way to Khartoum and into history. It is not surprising to find that he was deeply impressed by Gordon, whom he once described, with pardonable hyperbole, as the greatest English soldier who ever lived.[130]

The Sudan, by this time, had come under the sway of a fanatical religious leader, Mohammed Ahmed, known as the Mahdi, who had successfully resisted all attempts to re-establish Egyptian authority. The country was more trouble than it was worth to Britain, and it was decided that it should be abandoned. But, first, Egyptian garrisons and foreign nationals would have to be withdrawn, and this would be no easy matter. Travel through the vast wastes of this desert land was difficult in the most favourable circumstances, and the Mahdi would be unlikely to allow safe passage. That was why Gordon was sent to the Sudan, but his instructions were not clear - and he was a law unto himself. He made no attempt to arrange an evacuation, and before long he found himself besieged at Khartoum.

The Gordon Relief Expedition, in which Eddy took part, was delayed, first, by the British Government's procrastination and, secondly, by the preparations that had to be made by its commander, the recently ennobled General Lord Wolseley. The line of the Nile between the Sudan's border with Egypt and Khartoum forms the letter 'S'. The Expedition followed the river as far as Korti, a town that marks approximately the half-way point. There it divided into a River Column, which proceeded by steamer, and a Desert Column, which set off with camels and horses on land across the second bend of the 'S'. The two forces were to meet where the Desert Column struck the river again, at

Metemmeh, but if one missed the rendezvous the other was to go on alone.

Eddy joined the Desert Column, which was commanded by Colonel Sir Herbert Stewart. Also with the Desert Column was the head of the Intelligence Department of Wolseley's Staff, Colonel Sir Charles Wilson, and, according to one contemporary account of the Expedition, Eddy joined 'for service with Sir Charles Wilson in Khartoum'.[131] They made good progress at first, but they were attacked at the oasis of Abu Klea by a Mahdist horde, and though they beat off the dervishes they were able to do so only at great cost in terms of dead and wounded. Colonel Stewart's second-in-command, the dashing Colonel Frederick Burnaby, was killed. Abu Klea is one of the few battles in which a British square was broken, and it said to be the battle that Sir Henry Newbolt had in mind when he wrote *Vitaï Lampada*.[132]

> The sand of the desert is sodden red,-
> Red with the wreck of a square that broke;-
> The Gatling's jammed and the Colonel dead,
> And the regiment blind with dust and smoke.

The much weakened force had to fight the rest of its way to the rendezvous, and in one of the series of actions Colonel Stewart received a wound from which he died a few days later. Metemmeh was found to be in the hands of the Mahdists, and there was no sign of the River Column. With the deaths of Stewart and Burnaby, the command of the force had devolved on Sir Charles Wilson, who decided that they could not go on alone, but should take up a defensive position, at Gubat, near Metemmeh, in the area of the rendezvous, and wait for the River Column.

A few days later, as part of a plan made when communications were still open between Wolseley and Gordon, four steamers, which had been acting as privateers, arrived down river, to provide extra transport for the Relief Expedition, and they brought the news that Gordon could not hold out much longer. At this, Wilson moved. The steamers had all been badly damaged by enemy action, and he had two of them repaired. Then he set out for Khartoum, with the two steamers and a relief force of about two hundred and fifty men, including Eddy. They had been delayed by the repair work, and they were delayed further by shallow water and gunfire from the river banks; and the closer they came to Khartoum the clearer were the signs that they were too late. Eddy described the last scene in this act of the drama some years later, in a lecture at Highcliffe.[133]

> Having arrived within 400 yards of Khartoum, and seeing that the place was in the possession of the enemy and that no flag was flying upon the palace, they steamed down the Nile; and when they had gone twelve miles they sent messengers dressed in Mahdi uniform to ascertain the exact position of affairs. These returned with the report that Khartoum had fallen and that Gordon was killed.

But the fall of Khartoum and the death of Gordon, which took place on 26th January, 1885, was not the end of the drama for Eddy. Both Wilson's steamers struck rocks and were wrecked on their return journey, and it was he who ensured that the party was not left to the mercy of the Mahdists.

> Lieutenant Stuart-Wortley was dispatched to carry the news to Gubat in one of the two small boats, a felucca. He left at 6.45 p.m. (31st January), taking a crew of four English soldiers and eight natives. They were fired at and missed by the Wad Habeshi fort; and working splendidly, traversed the 40 miles in a little over eight hours, arriving at Gubat ... at 3 a.m. on the morning of 1st February. Stuart-Wortley and his men faced death every mile of the way; and their voyage deserves to be remembered as a bold, determined and gallant achievement.[134]

There was a brief diplomatic interlude for him in the summer of 1885, when he went to Constantinople as Military Attaché to Sir Henry Drummond Wolff, whose mission was to negotiate with Turkey on the future of Egypt; and it was presumably for his work with Sir Henry that he was appointed C.M.G. in 1886. Then, in Egypt again, he was D.A.A.G. and Q.M.G. to Sir Francis Grenfell, who had succeeded Sir Evelyn Wood as Sirdar, and he was present at the last action of the Sudanese campaign of 1884-1886. The Mahdists planned to invade Egypt, but at Ginnis, on the Sudanese side of the border, at the tail end of 1886, they were turned back. On successive days in 1886, Eddy was promoted Captain and Brevet-Major.

Regimental duties in England, to which he returned, must have seemed dull. In 1889, however, he was sent to the Staff College at Aldershot, and in 1891 he married. He married Violet Guthrie, whose father, James Guthrie, a Scot, 'came to London and sought the road to prosperity in stocks and shares'[135] - and evidently found it. Her mother, Elinor, was the daughter of Admiral Sir James Stirling, first Governor of New South Wales, and she was a beauty. She is said to have been the model for one of the Wise Virgins in Frederick, Lord Leighton's fresco *The Wise and Foolish Virgins*, in the Parish Church of St. Michael and All Angels at Lyndhurst. It was in 1891, too, that Eddy inherited Highcliffe.

His first Staff appointment after the course at the Staff College was as Brigade Major at Malta, where he spent the years 1893-1896 and must have had a complaisant General. When the Fleet paid an official visit to Venice, he and Violet went too, he with the Admiral in his flagship and she with the Admiral's wife in a yacht. And there were unofficial visits to Sicily, Corfu, Albania, Tunisia and Egypt. In Cairo, they dined with Lord Cromer, the former Sir Evelyn Baring, and Violet found him hard work. 'After dinner it was no better', she recorded. 'Sir Evelyn (sic) stood in front of the mantelpiece, his eyes on the clock. As it struck ten, he said "Good-night" firmly.'[136]

In 1896, the Sudan had acquired political and strategic importance in Africa, and Britain could no longer afford to leave the country in the hands of the Mahdists. Much else that was relevant to the situation had changed since the British withdrawal of 1885: the Kalifa Abdulla, who still ruled in the Sudan, could call on the support of hundreds of thousands of dervishes, but he could not command their loyalty as the Mahdi had commanded it; Cromer had rebuilt the Egyptian economy and re-formed the Egyptian Army; organisational changes had increased the efficiency of the British Army; and the British and Egyptian Armies had been equipped with modern weapons.

There followed, in the River War of 1896-1898, the reconquest of the Sudan by the Egyptian Army, reinforced by units of the British Army, under the command of the Sirdar, General Sir Herbert Kitchener. In the first phases of the war, a slow and cautious advance along the Nile to

Dongola and then to the Mahdist stronghold of Berber, fortunately abandoned by the Dervishes in the face of the advance, Eddy was on Kitchener's Staff. For some time, he was Staff Officer to the Gunboat Flotilla, the role of which was to reconnoitre, harass the enemy and provide artillery support in actions ashore. In the last phase of the war, culminating in the Battle of Omdurman, however, he particularly distinguished himself and won the D.S.O.

The assignment that gave him the opportunity so to distinguish himself was described by Winston Churchill, who was there.[137]

> While the army were to move along the west bank of the river - the Omdurman side - a force of Arab irregulars, formed from the friendly tribes, would march along the east bank and clear it of any Dervishes. All the debris which the Egyptian advance had broken off the Dervish Empire was thus to be hurled against that falling State. Eager for plunder, anxious to be on the winning side, Sheikhs and Emirs from every tribe in the Military Soudan had hurried, with what following the years of war had left them, to Wad Hamed. On 26th August (1898) the force of irregulars numbered about 2,500 men, principally Jaalin survivors, but also comprising bands and individuals of Bisharin; of Hadendoa from Suakin; of Shukria, the camel-breeders; of Batahin, who had suffered a bloody diminution at the Khalifa's hands; of Shaiggia, Gordon's vexatious allies; and lastly some Gemilab Arabs under a reputed son of Zubehr Pasha. The command of the whole motley force was given to Major Stuart-Wortley, Lieutenant Wood accompanying him as Staff Officer; and the position of these officers among the cowed and untrustworthy Arabs was one of considerable peril.

In his approach to Omdurman, where the Kalifa was known to be, Kitchener halted his army at a safe distance and sent the Gunboat Flotilla forward to bombard the city. The task of the irregulars, under Eddy, was to protect the gunboats' backs, and this entailed the storming of a number of enemy positions, which were fiercely defended. Of all the irregulars,

Major-General the Honourable Edward Stuart Wortley
by Archibald Stuart Wortley
Highcliffe Sports and Social Club

only the Jaalin showed much courage, but the combined operation was a success, and the bombardment persuaded the Kalifa to face Kitchener in the open desert, where the power of the Mahdists was finally broken. When the irregulars were disbanded, the Sheikh of the Jaalin gave Eddy a talisman that he had worn during the fighting, a turquoise pendant, which now belongs to the Royal Green Jackets Museum at Winchester.

Eddy's father, the Earl of Wharncliffe's younger brother and heir, had died in 1893, and when the Earl died in 1899 it was Eddy's elder brother who inherited the earldom. Eddy was treated as if his father had inherited first, however, and he was known thereafter as the Honourable Edward Stuart Wortley.

The Boer War was about power in South Africa, though the immediate cause was the Boers' inequitable treatment of immigrants and foreign workers - the Uitlanders - in the Transvaal. It lasted nearly three years, from 1899 to 1902, and it involved the British colonies of the Cape and Natal and the Boer republics of the Orange Free State and the Transvaal. The Commander-in-Chief of the British Army in South Africa at the beginning of the war was General Sir Redvers Buller, V.C., and Eddy, with the brevet rank of lieutenant-colonel, was on his Staff. Buller's original plan had been to invade the Orange Free State and the Transvaal from Cape Colony, raising the seiges of Kimberley and Mafeking on the way, but this would have left Natal in the hands of the Boers, who had Ladysmith under siege. Instead, he created separate commands and decided to go, himself, to Natal.

The Boers in Natal held a strong position behind the Tugela River and in the range of hills and mountains beyond, and Buller made three abortive attempts at breaking through, at Colenso, Spion Kop and Vaal Krantz, before, at the fourth attempt, he succeeded in doing so. After Colenso, however, he was superseded as Commander-in-Chief by Field-Marshal Lord Roberts, V.C., whose only son had been killed in the battle. Eddy was at the relief of Ladysmith, on 28th February, 1900, and at all the actions that led up to it, but we do not know much about the part that he played in them. Army Lists show that, though he was on the Staff, he raised and commanded a Volunteer Corps of Stretcher-Bearers, who were more reliable in the veld than army ambulances, and commanded a Battalion of Rifle Reservists. All that Violet adds to this information is the story that a hen called Emily laid an egg for his breakfast every morning at Spion Kop.

Eddy commanded the 2nd Battalion of the King's Royal Rifles for four months, from March to June, following the relief of Ladysmith, and it was in June that Buller, having outmanoeuvred the Boers at their border stronghold of Laing's Nek, advanced into the Transvaal. By this time, Roberts had moved up through the Orange Free State to the Transvaal; Kimberley and Mafeking had been relieved; and Bloemfontein, Johannesburg and Pretoria had surrendered. Now Roberts and Buller joined forces to deliver the *coup de grâce* to the Boers who had not surrendered, and by October they were sufficiently confident of their success to return to England. Eddy, back on the Staff, took part in a number of actions in the Orange Free State between June and October, and then he, too, returned to England. But it was not until May 1902 that all fighting ceased.

Eddy stood for Parliament, in a constituency in the West Riding of Yorkshire, in the so-called 'Khaki Election' of 1900, when the Government attempted to make capital out of the victory that was not yet a victory. He was in South Africa during the election campaign, and Violet did his canvassing for him. 'Great stress was laid on the brave fellow fighting for his country,' she wrote later, 'while his no less brave wife appealed for votes.'(138) The Government barely increased its majority and Eddy was not elected, but Violet was consoled by the fact that, in their constituency, the Conservatives increased their share of the vote at the expense of the Radicals, who held the seat.

A far cry from the battlefields of the Sudan and South Africa was the diplomatic scene at Paris, where he found himself next, from 1901 to 1904, as Military Attaché, with the substantive rank of lieutenant-colonel. It was an important moment in the history of Anglo-French relations: the moment of conception of the *Entente Cordiale*. France was in an intensely anti-British mood when Eddy arrived in 1901, which made the success of Edward VII's visit to Paris in 1903 particularly helpful and particularly surprising. The King, himself, was pleased, and among the tokens of his pleasure was the M.V.O. for Eddy.

Highcliffe had always been used to royal visits, and they did not cease with the death of Lady Waterford. When Eddy and Violet moved in, the house still had no bathrooms, no hot running water, no electric light and no central-heating, but this did not inhibit them from inviting the Duke and Duchess of Connaught and Strathearn to stay in the late autumn of 1892. The Duke was Queen Victoria's third son. He was a professional soldier, and the Colonel-in-Chief of Eddy's regiment, the King's Royal Rifle Corps. Next, in 1906, came King Alfonso of Spain, with a large party from the Isle of Wight, but they did not stay. Then, in 1907, by which time the domestic arrangements had been improved, the house was taken over at a week's notice by the Emperor William II of Germany and his suite, and there followed what must have been the most extraordinary episode in Eddy's life.

The Emperor spent three weeks at Highcliffe, on holiday, after a State visit to this country. He would deal with essential business in the mornings, and in the afternoons he would be driven, with his party, in a fleet of cars, to pay calls and visit places of interest in the locality. A photograph of him in a group at Kingston Lacey hangs inconspicuously in one of the bedrooms there. His own staff saw to most of his needs, but Mrs. Rosa Lewis, of the Cavendish Hotel in Jermyn Street, was brought in to cook for him. The local shops were unable to satisfy the demands of this remarkable woman, and she thought nothing of going up to London every day for her provisions, the Emperor's special train being at her disposal for the purpose.[139]

Relations between Britain and Germany, even at this time, were so bad that there was talk of war in some quarters. In discussions with Eddy, however, the Emperor expressed much pro-British feeling, and maintained that his greatest wish was for *rapprochement*. Some of his assurances may have failed to ring quite true, as when, in reply to a question that had a bearing on sea power, he said, 'But much as I have been misunderstood, I have built my fleet to support you.'[140] But Eddy was convinced of his sincerity. While he was at Highcliffe, the Emperor invited Eddy to watch the annual manoeuvres of the German Army with him the next year, and in Germany in 1908 there were more discussions, in which William returned to the same topics in the same terms.

The publication of the Emperor's views was now mooted, and these two oddly matched men agreed that nothing but good could come of it. Eddy prepared a report for the British press and submitted it to the Emperor for his approval and that of his Chancellor, Prince Bülow, and at this stage there was either misunderstanding or mischief. The report was returned to Eddy as if fully approved, it was published in *The Daily Telegraph* on 28th October, 1908, and - in the words of a diplomatic historian - it 'let loose a hurricane'.[141] The Emperor's Anglophile protestations were met with fury in Germany and scorn and derision in

England; and the violent wind caused damage, too, in countries less directly concerned. Bülow resigned, though not at once, and William's prestige was permanently impaired.

Eddy was on half-pay, that is unemployed, between 1904 and 1908. He was promoted brevet colonel in 1904, however, while he was still at Paris, and substantive colonel in 1907; and in 1906 he was appointed C.B. Then, in 1908, he was made a brigadier-general and given command of the 10th Infantry Brigade at Shorncliffe for four years. They were particularly happy years for the family, according to Violet. She and Eddy had three children: Rothesay, born in 1892; Louise, born in 1893; and Elizabeth, known as Bettine, born in 1896. Eddy became G.O.C. at Shorncliffe half way through the affair of the German Emperor, but his involvement in it did not become known until some time later, perhaps fortunately for him.

In the two years that led up to the First World War, 1912-1914, he was again on half-pay. He was promoted Major-General in 1913, and in 1914, shortly before the outbreak of war, he was given command of the North Midland Territorial Division. His regiment's journal, *The King's Royal Rifle Corps Chronicle*, provides a summary of his subsequent service.[142]

> He was selected for the command of the North Midland Territorial Division from June 1st, 1914, and so was in command of that Division on the outbreak of the Great War. His Division was the first in the Territorial Army to go, as a complete formation, to France, where it arrived in February 1915, becoming the 46th Division on joining the B.E.F. After a somewhat uneventful year in France, the Division was sent to Egypt to take part in the defence of the Suez Canal, but had no sooner arrived there than it was sent back to France. Stuart-Wortley remained in command of the Division till July, 5th, 1916, and a few months later took over command of the 65th Division in Ireland. He held this command till March 1918, and retired from the Army in July 1919.

The last phase of Eddy's life is the least well documented: Army Lists are no longer helpful, and Violet's books are less so than might be expected.

They travelled a great deal, revisiting Egypt at the end of 1929, and in 1932 retracing Lord Stuart de Rothesay's footsteps in Brazil. From Cairo, at the beginning of 1930, Eddy travelled on, at the invitation of the Governor of the Sudan, to Khartoum, where he spent the anniversary of Gordon's death. When they were at home, at Highcliffe, there was a constant flow of visitors, recorded in the Visitors' Book, which is preserved at the Victoria and Albert Museum. Queen Mary came to lunch one day, when the cook produced *crème de volaille* made of rabbit. Often, when they were away, Highcliffe was let, and Gordon Selfridge was their tenant for long periods of time between 1916 and 1925.[143]

Their only son, Rothesay, died of the complications of diabetes mellitus in 1926. He was at Eton and Oxford, and he was destined for a business career, on which he had embarked, in New York, when war broke out in 1914. He held Staff appointments in the early days of the war, first with the Territorial Division commanded by Eddy; but then he joined the Flying Corps, and he made a name for himself and won the M.C. as a fighter pilot. He married Marie Louise Edwardes, née Martin, a prima donna known as Madame Edvina, whose first husband had been killed in the war. He was unable to work once he became ill, but he was able to write, and he published articles on military aviation, stories for boys and a novel. The novel, *Letters from a Flying Officer*, based on his own experiences, was prefaced with a memoir of him by Duff Cooper and John Buchan.[144]

Louise married, in 1924, Sir Percy Loraine, Bart., a professional diplomat, at that time British Minister at Tehran. He was posted later, to Greece, Egypt and the Sudan, Turkey and, finally, as Ambassador, in 1939 and 1940, to Italy. In 1928, after a brief, unsuccessful, first marriage, Bettine married Montagu Bertie, who inherited the Earldom of Abingdon from his grandfather that same year, and the Earldom of Lindsey from a more distant relation ten years later. When first Rothesay and then Eddy died, Highcliffe became the property of Rothesay's wife,[145] but she had no wish to live there and she sold the estate to Lord Abingdon, who was its last private owner. Rothesay, Louise and Bettine all died childless.

Eddy died in 1934, in Morocco, where he had gone, with Violet, to avoid the English winter, but he was buried at Highcliffe, and the King's Royal Rifles provided full military honours. One of his obituarists gave it as his opinion that he - like Charles Stuart III - was more of an amateur than a professional soldier, thus explaining why his early promise was never fully realised.[146] The same writer thought he was more successful as a man than as a soldier.

> As a man, he was a very loveable person. He was generosity personified, a charming companion and a perfect host. There was nothing he would not do to help a friend, and that word includes everyone who served under him.

BIBLIOGRAPHY

Unpublished Sources
and Abbreviations

BL,O & IOC	British Library, Oriental and India Office Collection
CS	Charles Stuart, later Lord Stuart de Rothesay. Travels in Germany and the Imperial Hereditary States, 1796-1797. Journal in the possession of Lord Joicey.
DCRO	Dorset County Record Office
EUL	Edinburgh University Library. Papers of Sir Charles Stuart, Baron Stuart de Rothesay.
HCRO	Hampshire County Record Office
MSA	Mount Stuart Archives. Letters of the 2nd Marquess of Bute.
NLS	National Library of Scotland. Stuart de Rothesay Papers.
NMM	National Maritime Museum, Greenwich. Pitcairn Jones Warships Microfiche.
ONS,GRO	Office for National Statistics, General Register Office.
PRO	Public Record Office
RNM	Royal Naval Museum, Portsmouth. Documents.
SUL	Southampton University Library. Wellington Papers.
WCA	Winchester College Archives
WYA	West Yorkshire Archives. Canning Papers.

PUBLISHED SOURCES

Allen, Charles.
      A Glimpse of the Burning Plain, Michael Joseph, London, 1986

Anstruther, Ian.
      The Knight & the Umbrella, Geoffrey Bles, London, 1963

Ayling, Stanley.
      King George the Third, Collins, London, 1972

Benson, A.C. & Esher, The Viscount. (Ed.)
> The Letters of Queen Victoria, John Murray, London,
> 3 vols., 1908

Beresford, Admiral Lord Charles.
> Memoirs, Methuen & Co., London, 2 vols., 1914

Bryant, Sir Arthur.
> The Years of Endurance, Collins, London, 1942

Buddle Atkinson, R.H.M. & Jackson, G.A. (Ed.)
> Brougham & His Early Friends. Letters to James Loch, 1795-1809, published
> privately, London, 3 vols., 1908

Burke. (1)
> Commoners, 1st Ed., 1834-1838

Burke. (2)
> Peerage, 34th Ed., 1872

Canning, George.
> Corrected reports of speeches delivered by the Right Hon. George Canning,
> in the House of Commons, on December 12th, 1826, 2nd Ed., James Ridgway,
> London, 1827

Churchill, Winston S.
> The River War, Eyre & Spottiswoode, London, 1933

Craig, F.W.S. (Ed.)
> British Parliamentary Election Results, 1832-1885. 2nd Ed., Parliamentary
> Research Service, Dartmouth Publishing Company, Aldershot, 1989

Curzon of Kedleston, The Marquis.
> British Government in India, Cassell & Co., London, 2 vols., 1925

De Castro, J.Paul.
> The Gordon Riots, Oxford, 1926

Everett, Major-General Sir Henry.
> The History of the Somerset Light Infantry (Prince Albert's) 1685-1914,
> Methuen & Co., London, 1934

Fielding, Daphne.
> The Duchess of Jermyn Street, Eyre & Spottiswoode,
> London, 1964

Fortescue, Sir John.
> Six British Soldiers, Williams & Norgate, London, 1928

Franklin, Robert.
> Lord Stuart de Rothesay, Images, Upton-upon-Severn, 1993

Gurwood, Lieutenant-Colonel John. (Ed.)

        The Dispatches of Field Marshal the Duke of Wellington, John Murray,

        London, 12 vols., 1837

Hansard.

        Parliamentary Debates, 1846

Hare, Augustus J.C.

        The Story of Two Noble Lives, George Allen, London,

        3 vols., 1893

Highcliffe Parish Magazine, October 1892.

        (HCRO, 21M82.PZ5)

Home, The Honourable James A. (Ed.)

        Letters of Lady Louisa Stuart to Miss Louisa Clinton, Second Series,

        David Douglas, Edinburgh, 1903

Hunt, W.Holman.

        Pre-Raphaelitism & the Pre-Raphaelite Brotherhood, Macmillan & Co.,

        London, 2 vols., 1905

Jackson, Lady.

        The Court of the Tuileries, Richard Bentley & Son, London,

        2 vols., 1883

Joicey, Michael.

        The Lady Waterford Hall & Its Murals, Trustees of the Lady Waterford Hall,

        Ford, Northumberland, 1983

Jones, Raymond.

        The British Diplomatic Service, 1815-1914, Colin Smythe, Gerrards Cross, 1983

King's Royal Rifle Corps, The Chronicle of the

Longford, Elizabeth.

        Wellington - The Years of the Sword, Weidenfeld & Nicolson, London, 1969

Machado, Cândido Guinle de Paula. (Ed.)

        Sketchbook containing studies made in Brazil, 1825-1826, & associated

        documents, São Paulo, 1972

Maclagan, Michael.

        'Clemency' Canning, Macmillan & Co., London, 1962

Martin, Robert Bernard.

        Gerard Manley Hopkins, Flamingo, London, 1992

Maxwell, Sir Herbert. (Ed.)

        The Creevey Papers, John Murray, London, 1823

Medlam, Sarah.

    The Bettine, Lady Abingdon Collection, Victoria & Albert Museum, London, 1996

Millais, John Guille.

    The Life & Letters of Sir John Everett Millais, Methuen & Co.,

    2 vols., 1899

Mitford, Nancy. (Ed.)

    The Stanleys of Alderly, Chapman & Hall, London, 1939

Neville, H.M.

    Under a Border Tower, Mawson, Swan & Mawson, Newcastle-on-Tyne, 1896

Newall, Christopher.

    The Grosvenor Gallery Exhibitions, Cambridge, 1995

Newbolt, Sir Henry.

    Poems: New & Old, John Murray, 1914

Nicolas, Sir Nicholas. (Ed.)

    The Dispatches & Letters of Vice-Admiral the Lord Viscount Nelson,

    Henry Colburn, London, 7 vols., 1844-1846

Nicoullaud, M.Charles. (Ed.)

    Memoirs of the Comtesse de Boigne, 1781-1814, Heinemann, London, 3 vols., 1907

Pocock, Tom.

    Horatio Nelson, Pimlico, London, 1994

Pound, Reginald.

    Selfridge, Heinemann, London, 1960

Salsbury, Henry.

    Highcliffe Castle - A History & Guide, The Catholic Records Press, Exeter, 1960

Schweizer, Karl W. (Ed.)

    Lord Bute - Essays in Re-interpretation, Leicester University Press, 1988

Sedgwick, Romney. (Ed.)

    Letters from George III to Lord Bute, 1756-1766, Macmillan & Co., London, 1939

Smith, David Benner. (Ed.)

    Letters of Admiral of the Fleet the Earl of St. Vincent, printed for the Navy Records

    Society, London, 2 vols., 1927

Stapleton, Edward J. (Ed.)

    Some Official Correspondence of George Canning, 1820-1827,

    Longmans Green & Co., London, 2 vols., 1887

Stuart (1), General Charles.

    Short Sketch of the Life of Louisa, Marchioness of Waterford, Spottiswoode & Co.,

    London, 1892

Stuart (2), Lieutenant-Colonel Charles.

Journal of a Residence in Northern Persia & the Adjacent Provinces of Turkey, Richard Bentley, London, 1854

Stuart Wortley, Rothesay.

Letters from a Flying Officer, Oxford, 1928

Stuart Wortley (1), Violet.

Magic in the Distance, Hutchinson & Co., London, 1948

Stuart Wortley (2), Violet.

Highcliffe & the Stuarts, John Murray, London, 1927

Stuart Wortley (3), Violet.

A Prime Minister & His Son, John Murray, London, 1925

Stuart Wortley (4), Violet.

Life Without Theory, Hutchinson & Co., London, 1946

Stuart Wortley (5), Violet.

Grow Old Along With Me, Secker & Warburg, London, 1952

Surtees (1), Virginia.

Charlotte Canning, John Murray, London, 1975

Surtees (2), Virginia. (Ed.)

Sublime & Instructive, Michael Joseph, London, 1972

Times (1).

The Christchurch

Times (2).

The (London)

Ward, Sir A.W. & Gooch, G.P.

The Cambridge History of British Foreign Policy, 1783-1919, Cambridge, 3 vols., 1923

Watts, M.S.

George Frederic Watts, Macmillan & Co., 3 vols., London, 1912

Woodham-Smith, Cecil.

The Great Hunger, Hamish Hamilton, London, 1962

Wraxall, Sir N. William.

Historical Memoirs of My Own Time, Kegan, Paul, Trench, Trubner & Co., London, 1904

REFERENCES

Introduction

1.   Stuart Wortley (1) p.234
2.   Stuart Wortley (2) p.7

The Earl Of Bute

3.   Wraxall
4.   Sedgwick
5.   Ayling, p.71
6.   Schweizer, p.57
7.   Ibid, p.254
8.   Ibid, p.170
9.   Stuart Wortley (2) p.15

General Sir Charles Stuart

10.   Stuart Wortley (3) p.108
11.   Ibid, p.183
12.   De Castro, p.185
13.   Fortescue, p.159
14.   Ibid, p.164
15.   Ibid, p.169
16.   Stuart Wortley (3) p.312
17.   Fortescue, p.171
18.   Bryant, p.297

Lord Stuart de Rothesay

19.   Buddle Atkinson, p.275
20.   Franklin, p.96
21.   Gurwood, v.9, p.452
22.   Stuart Wortley (2) p.193
23.   Longford, p.416
24.   Stuart Wortley (2) p.235 (footnote)

25.   Maxwell, p.236

26.   NLS, MS.6164, p.727

27.   NLS, MS.6320

28.   Jones, p.57

29.   NLS, MS.6171

30.   CS

31.   Salsbury, p.44

32.   Stapleton, v.1, p.155

33.   Machado

34.   Stuart Wortley (2) p.185 (footnote)

35.   WYA

36.   SUL, WP1/895/20

37.   Maxwell, p.486

38.   SUL, WP1/1137/43

39.   Hare, v.1, p.197

Captain John Stuart R.N.

40.   PRO, ADM.107.24

41.   WCA

42.   PRO, ADM.107.24

43.   Stuart Wortley (2)

44.   EUL, Dk.6.25.[1-7]

45.   Stuart Wortley (3) p.267

46.   EUL, Dk.6.25. [5]

47.   Stuart Wortley (3) p.288

48.   EUL, Dk.6.25.[2]

49.   Ibid

50.   Nicolas, v.5, p.169

51.   Smith, v.2, p.264

52.   Ibid. p.317

53.   RNM, 56/111(1)

54.   Stuart Wortley (2) p.65

55.   Pocock, p.317

56.   Nicolas, v.7, p.49

57.   Stuart Wortley (2) p.67

58.   Burke (1) p.410

59.   Burke (2) p.167

60.   Hare, v.3, p.386

61. Stuart Wortley (2) p.122
62. NMM, *Clyde* of 1796
63. Stuart Wortley (2) p.170

Lady Canning

64. Jackson, v.2, p.267
65. Nicoullaud, v.3, p.174
66. Surtees (1) p.71
67. Benson, v.3, p.475
68. Hare, v.2, p.478
69. Medlam, p.81
70. Surtees (1) p.92
71. BL,O&IOC, Mss Eur D661
72. Maclagan, p.20
73. Surtees (1) p.193
74. Maclagan, p.46
75. Hare, v.2, p.73
76. Curzon, v.2, p.227
77. Mitford, p.214
78. BL,O& IOC, Mss Eur D661
79. Allen, p.149
80. Maclagan, p.306

Lady Waterford

81. Hare, v.1, p.192
82. Anstruther, p.197
83. Hare, v.1, p.231
84. Watts, v.1, p.98
85. Hare, v.3, p.240
86. Surtees (2) p.15
87. Ibid, p.12
88. Hunt, v.1, p.350
89. Neville, p.81
90. Millais, v.1, p.364
91. Neville, p.85
92. Woodham-Smith, p.298
93. Hansard, 1846, v.85, col.1076
94. Hare, v.1, p.326

95.   Ibid, v.3, p.463

96.   Joicey, p.9

97.   Newall, p.3

98.   Ibid, p.24

99.   Neville, p.86

100.   Joicey, p.8

101.   Hare, v.3, p.443

102.   Ibid, v.3, p.470

103.   Ibid, v.3, p.476

104.   Stuart (1) p.30

105.   Watts, v.2, p.203

General Charles Stuart (Charles Stuart III)

106.   EUL, Dk.6.25.[9]

107.   Canning, p.39

108.   Home, p.43 & 53

109.   MSA

110.   Craig

111.   Home, p.535

112.   Stuart (2)

113.   Ibid, p.346

114.   EUL, Dk.6.25.[25]

115.   Everett, p.222-227

116.   Highcliffe Parish Magazine, October 1892

117.   DCRO, D/V1Z/17

118.   Maclagan, p.207

119.   Hare, v.3, p.51

120.   Mitford, p.219

121.   *Times (2)*, 18th May, 1861

122.   Martin, p.121

123.   *Times (1)*, 10th December, 1892

124.   Highcliffe Parish Magazine, October 1892

125.   Ibid.

126.   *Times (1)*, 10th December, 1892

General Edward Stuart Wortley

127.   Hare, v.3, p.466

128.   Stuart Wortley (4)

129.   Stuart Wortley (5)

130.   *Times (1)*, 12th March, 1892

131.   Beresford, p.256

132.   Newbolt, p.78

133.   *Times (1)*, 12th March, 1892

134.   Beresford, p.294

135.   Stuart Wortley (5) p.14

136.   Stuart Wortley (4) p.30

137.   Churchill, p.249

138.   Stuart Wortley (5) p.78

139.   Fielding, p.72

140.   Stuart Wortley (5) p.101

141.   Ward, v.3, p.391

142.   *King's Royal Rifle Corps Chronicle*, 1934, p.178

143.   Pound

144.   Stuart Wortley, Rothesay

145.   ONS, GRO, Will of Rothesay Stuart Wortley

146.   *King's Royal Rifle Corps Chronicle*, 1934, p.178

INDEX

Isabella, The Infanta. 26, 69

Italy. 63, 72, 78, 92

J

Jaalin. 86, 88

Jackson, Lady. 42

James, Henry. 67

Jervis, Admiral Sir John. See The Earl of St. Vincent

Johannesburg. 89

John VI, King of Portugal. See also the Prince Regent of Portugal. 23, 25

Johnson, Samuel. 7

Joicey, Lord. 64

Josephine, The Empress. 19

Jubbulpore. 53

K

Kabul. 81

Kaiser, The. See William II, German Emperor

Kandahar. 81

Kenwood House, London. 8

Kew Gardens. 7

Kew Green. 8

'Khaki Election', The. 89

Khartoum. 82 et seq., 92

Khedive, The. (of Egypt) 81

Kimberley. 88, 89

Kingston Lacey, Dorset. 90

Kitchener (Horatio Herbert), Field Marshal the Earl. 85 et seq.

Knowles, Captain Sir Charles, Bart. 32

Korti. 82

L

Labour Rate Act, The. 61

Ladysmith. 88, 89

Lady Waterford Hall, Ford, Northumberland. 67

Lahore. 52

Landseer, Charles. 23, 46

Landseer, Sir Edwin. 23

113

Stuart, Charles (II). See Lord Stuart de Rothesay

Stuart, (Charles III). General Charles Stuart. 2, 7, 26, 40, 50, 52, 66, 68 et seq., 92

Stuart, The Honourable Charlotte. See the Viscountess and Countess Canning

Stuart, Georgiana. (Minny). The Honourable Mrs. (Charles III) Stuart. 50 et seq., 72 et seq.

Stuart, John. See the 3rd Earl of Bute

Stuart, Captain John, R.N. 2, 31 et seq., 68

Stuart (Louisa), The Honourable Lady. 9, 34, 38, 40, 42

Stuart, The Honourable Louisa. See the Marchioness of Waterford

Stuart, Louisa. The second Mrs. Charles Stuart (III). 78

Stuart de Rothesay (Elizabeth), Lady. 1, 20, 21, 29, 42 et seq., 52, 55, 63

Stuart de Rothesay, Lord. (Charles Stuart II). 1, 15 et seq., 31, 32, 40, 42, 45, 55, 68, 70, 74, 92

Stuart Wortley, Major-General the Honourable Edward. 1, 80 et seq.

Stuart Wortley, Elizabeth. Known as Bettine. Later Countess of Abingdon. 1, 91

Stuart Wortley, Louise. Later Lady Loraine. 1, 91, 92

Stuart Wortley, Marie Louise. Mrs. Rothesay Stuart Wortley. 92

Stuart Wortley, Rothesay. 1, 91, 92

Stuart Wortley, Violet. The Honourable Mrs. Edward Stuart Wortley. 85 et seq.

Sudan, The. 81 et seq., 92

Sullivan, Albinia. See Albinia Stuart. (Mrs. John Stuart)

Sullivan, The Right Honourable John. 39, 68

Suez Canal. 81, 82, 91

Swilly, Lough. 41

Switzerland. 71, 78

T

Taj Mahal. 52

Talma. 22

Tankerville, The Countess of. 66

Tate Gallery, The, London. 67

Tehran. 71, 92

Tel-el-Kebir. 82

Territorial Division, The North Midland. 91, 92

Thompson, Honoria. 66

Thompson, The Reverend Marmaduke. 69

Tilsit. 16

Tintoretto. 57

Tipperary. 60

Titian. 57